A
CATHOLIC
LIFE

A CATHOLIC LIFE

GERALD MURPHY

Matador
9 Priory Business Park,
Wistow Road, Kibworth Beauchamp,
Leicestershire. LE8 0RX
Tel: (+44) 116 279 2299
Fax: (+44) 116 279 2277
Email: books@troubador.co.uk
Web: www.troubador.co.uk/matador

ISBN 978 1788035 828

British Library Cataloguing in Publication Data.
A catalogue record for this book is available from the British Library.

Printed by TJ International Ltd, Padstow, Cornwall
Typeset in 12pt Bembo by Troubador Publishing Ltd, Leicester, UK

Matador is an imprint of Troubador Publishing Ltd

To all my friends in Serra

CONTENTS

Foreword

This is not an autobiography in the normal sense of the word. My diaries contain only dates and times of meetings. My memory has never been good and it is even less reliable today. I do, however, enjoy telling stories about incidents in my life, and the telling has imprinted them on my memory. Because some of them are unusual, friends encouraged me to write a book. At first, I feared the task was going to take forever, until I realised that a book could be used to attract donations for the work of Serra. This focused my attention and spurred me on. Serra has been the most dominant influence in my life.

Part of me also thought that reflecting about my life might answer two questions I have frequently been asked, and have often asked myself. Why did I never put myself forward for the priesthood, and why did it take me 75 years to get to marriage, which is so important to me now? This book has helped me see the close relationship between my religion, architecture and the community, but I still cannot answer those questions. Perhaps when you have read it you will be able to answer them for me.

CHAPTER 1

My Family

My family was small: just father, mother, and my younger brother. But who they were and what they achieved had a great influence on my life.

My father was the third of eleven children, born in the largest house in Athea, a small town in the south west of Ireland. It was not just their home. It was also the police station, the symbol of authority in the area, and my grandfather was the policeman. This must have made it very difficult for my father to decide to join the Irish Republican Army during the war for Irish Independence, but he did and was shot in the thigh while driving a motor bike and sidecar with a gun mounted on it. Because attending an Irish hospital would have led to his capture he was smuggled across the sea to Liverpool and hospitalised there. By the time he was fit enough to go back, 'the troubles' were over and the IRA had no further use for him. He would not have been welcome at home. Everyone wanted the independence, but few believed that it should have been fought for, something that was especially true of those, like my grandfather, who worked for the Irish establishment. Eventually, everyone came to accept the different approaches to gaining independence, and Ireland is full of examples of how well they came to terms with it. Pieces of land where people of both nationalities were killed are still protected by railings, and not farmed. There is a war memorial erected by the Irish just outside Youghal that recognises their men who died on one side and the English on the other. They are able to blame the government and the army without blaming the English people.

England was not an easy place to find work during those years, for it was scarce and the Irish were not particularly welcome. Father's lack of education was also a problem. After several years of casual employment he gave up his reluctance to work for the British Crown and joined the Metropolitan police. It was easy enough to join but he had to take a correspondence course in reading, writing and arithmetic to pass the examination for sergeant. He finally reached the rank of Chief Inspector with responsibility for the police in cars and on bikes in one eighth of London. In those days there were more policemen on motor bikes than in cars and he was able to use his experience with motor bikes to train his men to high standards. Indeed, he actually formed a team to give displays for special occasions. When D Day approached they were called upon to outride the troops travelling though London to the coast. This movement was carried out at night when the lights on the vehicles were heavily shielded. Taking the trucks through the unlit Thames tunnels was particularly dangerous, but none of his men was injured and his active leadership of the operation was highly commended. He was a good policeman but he was motivated principally by the need to earn a living for his family and a desire to prepare for his retirement. By the time he reached it, his health was poor and he succumbed to angina. He lived just long enough to see me qualified but not long enough to enjoy the house I had designed for his retirement.

It was several years before father was accepted by his family in Ireland. He had to overcome the position he had taken during the war, and his marriage to an English protestant. By the time he eventually took mother to visit the family she had converted to Catholicism and they liked her as a person. From then on he visited Ireland frequently and only stopped when his health failed.

My strongest memory of father was of the night my brother and I returned very late home to our bungalow in Potters Bar. We had walked the last three miles from the wreck of father's brand new Triumph Mayflower. My brother Derek had failed to see an unlit stationary van on the hill just outside Potters Bar. He swerved to miss the van but failed to see an oncoming vehicle. He managed to avoid a head-on collision but the combination of swerve and partial impact sent us through a hedge into the adjoining field. Fortunately, no one was hurt and we exchanged details with the driver of the other car. We walked home wondering how we could explain the possible 'write-off' to father. He was a strict disciplinarian but easy to love. By the time we reached home he was asleep. When we woke him, all he was interested in was our state of health. When he was satisfied that we were unharmed he said we should leave decisions about the car till the morning, and went back to sleep.

I was very proud of what my father had achieved and he was responsible for my feeling as Irish as I do English. I also had no difficulty in supporting his right to join the IRA in their fight for independence, and am satisfied that they would not have achieved independence at that time without the war. I did not, however, support the IRA in the Northern Irish troubles in the 1970s and '80s because I am just as convinced that they could have achieved the same result by political means.

My mother was one of the five children born to a building construction foreman. Unfortunately, he died before I was old enough to remember him but 'Gran' was still living in Stockmar Road, Hackney, where mother was born, and I still remember the scullery with its stone copper for washing the clothes and the earthenware sink for washing up. Cooking was done on a coal-burning iron range in the living room; this was also the only form of heating in the house. I loved to watch Gran's lodger keeping his feet warm in the oven while reading the newspaper. He was the stage doorman at the Hackney Empire and sometimes took my brother and me backstage to watch the show. They had many different variety acts, but by far the most exciting were the conjurers. I enjoyed trying to see how they managed to fool the audience; it was a little easier to see how they did it from backstage.

Mother went to elementary school until she was fourteen. She then joined the 'Hello girls', the first telephone operators, and was trained to speak 'properly'. She met father at a dance in his Section House, where single policemen lived. She gave up work when I was expected and only went back when my brother and I started at boarding school. When war broke out she became a food officer, controlling the rationing of food. Her knowledge of the rationing system encouraged her to move from working in the Town Hall to renting a grocery corner shop just off Priory Road in Hornsey. This did much to improve the quality of the family's diet. After the war the shop was sold and mother became senior credit manager at the John Lewis store in Oxford Street, where she remained until they asked her to control credit in a new shop north of London. When she told them she was not prepared to leave London they dismissed her. She challenged the decision but to no avail. She then joined the administration of the Nursing Council until her retirement at the age of seventy. She lived a further twenty-seven healthy years happily gardening, first at home and then at her warden assisted flat in Muswell Hill.

When she was ninety I gave her a party, and invited ninety of her friends and relatives. One of them organised a subscription to purchase a pair of tickets to travel on the Orient Express. She chose to be accompanied by a niece but remained very much in charge. Even later, she travelled to Toronto on her own to visit her nephew Dan and his family. She stayed fit until her death at ninety-seven. Her will required me to have her buried in Highgate Cemetery because she wanted me to visit her grave more often than we had managed to visit those of my father and brother in Potters Bar.

We had lived apart from the time I left college, sometimes in flats within the same building, but never more than three miles from each other. I loved my mother and we were able to support one another after the deaths of my father and brother. She did the ironing and I did the household repairs. I enjoyed involving her in my social life and she enjoyed being involved. She accompanied me to many of the conventions and social gatherings I attended, but living apart diminished the control she wanted to have over my life. We were each able to retreat to our own space.

My brother, Derek, was born twenty-one months after me. This was fortunate. I do not think I would have enjoyed being the younger brother but he did not seem to mind. It was important at boarding school because the elder is expected to be responsible for the younger; we did most things together until I left school. Derek then went into the sixth form and left with a good higher school certificate. He joined the Unilever management scheme until his 'call up'. When it came he was given the chance of going before the War Office Selection Board. They liked him and he was trained to be an officer in the Royal Army Service corps. He loved the life. The travelling abroad and the sports were particularly appealing to him. He excelled in every form of sport, team and solo, achieving national standard for the Army in the hammer and shot put, the pentathlon and the skiing biathlon.

After two years' service he returned to Unilever, but after missing army life for only six months he applied to go to the Royal Military Academy at Sandhurst. He was accepted, passed out well, and offered a permanent commission in a Guards regiment. He was tempted, but returned to his first love, The Royal Army Service Corps – a fortunate choice because I was supplementing his income at this time. He became a very effective officer and received early promotions to captain and major. He was expecting to be made up to half colonel when, in 1970, he had reason to go for tests to the military hospital at Millbank. After a week he was told that he was 100 per cent fit, and the family celebrated the news with a glass of sherry. That evening he returned to duty on the night sleeper. When the train arrived at Plymouth, however, he was found dead in his bunk. He had died in his sleep of coronary artery atheroma. He was only thirty-seven.

The nearly two years difference in age, together with my feeling very responsible for my younger brother at boarding school, tended to separate us at school, and I think we would have preferred not to have been brothers. However, when I next spent time with him during his leave from the army we thoroughly enjoyed each other's company. We particularly enjoyed introducing one another to our different lifestyles. About the only thing we had in common was that we were both still single. I miss him very much. He was a fine man and I was very proud of him.

CHAPTER 2

My left leg

I was born in 1931 when my parents were living in the area of the original toll gate at the bottom of Highgate Hill. The actual road was eliminated during the Second World War and is now a housing estate.

I appeared to be a normal child until the time came for me to start walking. I couldn't stand up. I crawled with one leg tucked under me, while the other leg dragged me forward. My parents took me to the GP who sent me to hospital where the leg in question was found to be too weak to support me and leg irons were proposed. When they were fitted it became apparent that the same leg was also much shorter than the other one. I therefore needed a pair of boots with one heel raised as well as the leg irons.

I wore the irons until my left leg was stronger – I can't remember for how long but I certainly did not have them when I started school. The difference in length, however, became greater as I grew taller. It had become a fraction short of two inches by the time I had stopped growing. The wedge in the shoe sloped from a quarter of an inch at the toe to two inches at the heel and I had a pronounced limp

My father went to great lengths to investigate the possibilities of my walking without the raised boot. The only answer suggested by orthodox medicine was to break the long leg and leave it broken on several occasions until the short one caught up. This would have meant losing a great deal of schooling and my parents felt that was unacceptable. I got accustomed to the boot and although it stopped me entering most sports there were compensations: I worked extra hard at the sports I could manage and became very good at fencing and archery. I particularly remember the thrill I got in my mid-teens when there was a fashion for playing all kinds of games on stilts. I made mine of different lengths to compensate for the difference in my legs and was able to use them as well as any of my friends. I could even play football.

The solution I eventually accepted resulted from a conversation my father had with the Arsenal osteopath, whom he had met while on duty at the football matches. He suggested moving the two inch difference further up my bone structure by creating a curved spine on a tilted pelvis. This was only possible while I was still growing. It became even easier as I grew to six foot four inches. To achieve this a programme was devised consisting of various exercises and a great deal of walking. I was trained to walk with a kind of spring in my step that was not obvious. When the war was over and I ceased to be a boarder, my father was able to take me for walks and make sure I was doing everything properly. By the time I left school at sixteen I could do it without thinking, and my shoulders were quite level. When I sat down one knee was a little over an inch higher than the other but the remainder of the two inches between knee and hip was less noticeable and almost nobody was aware of my problem. Occasionally, when I am very tired and cannot concentrate on my spring, people have noticed me limping, but it never occurs to them that I have one leg two inches longer than the other. From then on I ceased to think that I was physically disadvantaged; I was the same as everyone else.

I was so sure that I could hide it from everyone that I tried to pass the medical for compulsory military service. The various subject specialists were seated in a series of bays formed by screens at one end of a school assembly hall. We were placed in a line, visiting each specialist in turn. In front of me was a very anaemic lad who was trying to get the specialists to read his doctor's letter describing his condition. Each one ignored his letter and passed him onto the next specialist. I appeared to be doing very well until I got to the last bay. The specialist told the anaemic lad to wait to one side and asked me to lift my right leg up sideways as far as I could. He then asked me to do the same thing with my left leg. I immediately realised I was in trouble. Because of my tilted pelvis I could not lift the left leg as high as the right one. Had I not tried so hard to lift my right leg as high as I could, I might possibly have got away with it. He said he knew there was something wrong and I should tell him what it was. I avoided the question and explained that my army brother had told me that if I could pass fully fit there was a good chance of my getting a commission but if they knew what was wrong I would probably be passed fit enough to serve, without a commission, in a non-combatant role. The Army doctor was not impressed, however, and insisted on an explanation of my problem. When he had heard the full history of my legs he decided to leave the decision to the Medical Officer in charge and conducted me and the anaemic to the Chief Medical Officer who was seated at a desk in the centre of the hall. All the specialists involved gathered around us. The stories of the anaemic trying to get out and my trying to get in were told. After some discussion the anaemic lad was told that the army would be good for him and he was passed fit. When he left I was told that the army had gained a recruit they might not have been entitled to but that I should go out and start earning my living. Now that the war was over there was a greater need for architects to make good the war damage than there was for recruits in the army. The MO did, however, warn me to be careful of my back, saying that the solution I had adopted would leave me with a weakness which could cause me trouble as I grew older. He has still to be proved right.

The only time my back caused me trouble was when I fell three floors from some scaffolding. I was stepping across a gap between the scaffold and an opening in the existing building. As it was near where I lived I had popped in on my way home and the light at that time of day was not very good. When I missed my footing I tried hard to avoid any projections on the way down, and so fell in a rigidly upright position onto some concrete paving. I remained conscious but the pain I experienced was so extreme I thought I had injured my spine. At least, that was where the pain was focused; its intensity made me sure I had broken something. Fortunately, the site manager was waiting for me to leave and heard my call. He wanted to get me to lie down but I insisted he left me standing, holding onto the scaffolding, until the ambulance arrived. The ambulance took me to the Whittington Hospital where I had several X-rays. The spine had certainly taken a shunt but nothing appeared broken. They told me to return the next morning when the X-rays would have dried and a consultant would be available to provide a more thorough diagnosis. I was given tablets to quell the pain and felt much better. An ambulance took me home. When I got to my flat I walked unaided up the front steps and put myself to bed where I slept very well. In the morning, my alarm went off and I started to get out of bed. My back was fine but as soon as I put my foot on the floor I screamed in agony. Something was very wrong.

I managed to crawl to a phone for an ambulance to take me back to the hospital where it was discovered that the ankle on the short leg had taken the worst of the landing and was badly broken. The long leg had suffered only some fine hairline cracks. The medical staff put the short leg in plaster and bound the long leg, while a doctor explained that the nerves in the spine were closer to the brain than those in the foot, so that messages from that region took precedence over those from lower down, which was why the injury to my foot had been overlooked.

After further examination of the vertebrae it was discovered that some of these had been squeezed and might cause problems in the future. For several years I did get back ache if I stood for any length of time and I had to put up with this during the years we architects stood to work on drawing boards. It ceased when we converted to computers.

The fall also gave me other problems. It had happened close to Christmas and it was difficult to avoid standing for long periods of time as there were parties and pub celebrations. The leg started to swell. I returned to the hospital where they were able to ease the plaster a little. Then came an office party in a French restaurant near Leicester Square. It had become famous for good food, but was better known as the restaurant where women did everything. They not only owned it, they did the cooking and the waiting on tables – unheard of in those days. We were put in the basement where the bench seating in an overcrowded area made movement impossible. The leg felt as if it were continuing to swell and remained uncomfortable over Christmas, but I put up with it. However, I decided to go back to hospital immediately after the holiday.

In the early hours of Boxing Day morning I was being driven back from a party by my brother. As we drove up Dartmouth Park Hill and were about to pass the Whittington Hospital he stopped and announced that he was going to take me into A & E there and then and avoid having to get up early in the morning. The A & E department was strangely quiet, the only person in sight being a young doctor reading a book. She put me on an inspection couch and cut the plaster off. The leg was badly swollen, and she was not certain what to do next, so she left me to seek another opinion and returned with three other young doctors. Their manner and dress gave me the impression that they had been pulled out of a party. One of them put his finger into the flesh; it went in about half an inch and when he withdrew it the indentation remained.

I was reminded of a film in which Sydney Greenstreet played an evil plantation owner. In one scene he is sitting on his veranda on a hot day displaying the effects of some awful tropical disease and surrounded by his workers who are wondering whether he is too ill to continue to be a problem to them. One of them, probably Peter Lorre, puts his finger into the swollen leg with a result identical to that which I had just seen on my own leg. He declares that the disease has really taken hold and Greenstreet is dying.

The doctor with the finger said I had phlebitis and the others agreed. The doctor on duty then fitted a cannula and pumped in the first of many doses of a blood thinning agent. The leg was left in the bottom half of the plaster for support and I was taken up to a ward that was covered in Christmas decorations.

After two weeks, the swelling had gone down and the leg was reset in a new plaster. This enabled me to walk again, though with crutches. I was also able to work by using Derek, a junior assistant architect from the office, as my chauffeur, an arrangement which lasted for the best part of a year. I had to wait not only until the ankle was set, but also for a further six months whilst I attended the Whittington every Wednesday to learn how to walk again. The fact that it was my short leg that had sustained the more serious injury made rehab a slow process.

The following winter I went skiing in Austria and after a few days the ankle of the short leg started to swell again. I tried to ignore it and relied on the ski boots to hold me. They did for a while but the day came when the ankle was no longer able to support me, even in ski boots. Of course, this had to happen when I was close to the summit so I was treated to a very fast trip straight down on the mountain ambulance. This, if you have not seen one, resembles a metal canoe. It is manoeuvred by two ambulance skiers, one pulling from the front, the other acting as a brake at the back. I was laid in the canoe with my head at the front and treated to the strange experience of not being able to see where I was going but only where I had been. The speeds these vehicles reach are high and it was more frightening than almost anything else I have experienced. My left ankle still gets swollen if I am on it too long, but it has never prevented me doing what I wanted to do – apart from skiing.

CHAPTER 3

School

My first school was St Martha's, a small convent school in Barnet with the playground between the school and the pavement. I have a vague recollection of playing in that playground but this may well be because I often drive past the children in the same playground today.

My second school was in Eire and my most vivid recollection of that school is also connected with the playground. It was of my brother and me standing in three square feet of it during playtime. This area was clearly marked out in white paint at St Canice's, a Christian Brothers School in Dublin. We had to stand in this square until we were able to speak Gaelic. All the subjects were taught in Gaelic, even English. The Christian Brothers have suffered much criticism in recent times for this kind of cruelty but I have to accept that we learnt Gallic very quickly.

When we were able to return to England, some eighteen months later, the bombing in London was severe. My parents were anxious to find a boarding school situated outside the centre of London, but close enough for them to visit us regularly. They chose Finchley Catholic Grammar School and I entered the Junior Prep. Canon Clement Parsons, the headmaster, allowed Derek to live with us at the school but for lessons he was taken to St Michael's Convent, a school about half a mile away, where he remained until he was old enough to enter the Grammar School. The school was founded by the canon in 1902 when he was parish priest at St Alban's Church in North Finchley. There was no Catholic school for boys in the area, and with the help of friends and parishioners he decided to start one. He purchased a large, impressive, Victorian castellated property on several acres of land called The White House. Because the canon wanted the school to be a public school, he also purchased another large property on the periphery of the school site which he called Feckenham, after the last abbot of Westminster. This enabled him to take boarders. The application to become a public school, however, was still being considered when the Second World War broke out and the war put a stop to his plans. By the time we entered, it had become a Grammar School.

Most of my time I lived in Feckenham House, but as the number of boarders grew, Canon Parsons had to find other accommodation. I spent a year with three boys living in Feckenham but sleeping in the house next to the school, which housed the canon's mother. This was a great escape from dormitory life. We were allowed to listen to 'The Man in Black' on the radio instead of on homemade crystal sets smuggled into the dormitory. At the end of the year we slept in a room on the first floor of The White House. This had become the head offices of the school, and contained the living accommodation and offices of the staff, the school dining room and the chapel. Four of us slept there as sacristan and altar servers to the priest members of staff. The only prize I achieved at speech day was a book for being a sacristan.

I was a very average student at everything except Religious Instruction and Art. I had great difficulty in absorbing information. I have since learnt that I am partially dyslexic, and this may well have created the difficulties. I did, however, manage, by spending a great deal of time memorising the work, to leave with five credits and my 'Matric'. I wanted to be an architect and I was anxious to leave school and start my training. In the fifth year we had a 'careers day' where I was told by a lady interviewer that I was not in the best school for preparing someone for a career in architecture because art was not its strong point. She also told me that nine places in every ten were being allotted to ex-servicemen. I should, therefore, give up any idea of being an architect and choose something else. I owe a great deal to that lady, because her advice made me even more committed to my choice.

Another incident that, though it questioned my ability, also strengthened my resolve was my being reported to the Head for cheating in an art exam. The subject had been to draw a freehand pattern. I was accused of having used a ruler to draw the lines. I explained that I was able to draw straight lines by using the edge of the desk as a guide to the palm of my hand. Mrs Hamilton, the art mistress (with no qualifications in art) was not impressed. She insisted that I must have used a ruler. She said that she thought I should be expelled and reported me to the Canon. I was so upset when I went up to the Head's study, I was unable to draw the straight line he asked for. I broke down, and cried. I think he understood the position because he did not punish me.

There was, however, another occasion when I nearly did get expelled. I was reported by a prefect for missing mass and being in a toilet compartment in the lavatory block with two other boys. We explained that we were learning some English prose by heart, for the master taking the class after mass. I was not aware, at that time, that there was another more serious interpretation of these facts, and was surprised when the Head told us we would be expelled. There were always boys in the toilets dodging class. When the head prefect learnt of our punishment, he must have realised that the facts had been misunderstood because he went at once to the head and explained that it was not unusual for boys to hide in the toilets. On the day in question there had been other boys in the toilets missing the same class but they had escaped while he was taking our names. The expulsion was revoked. It was not until many years after the incident that I understood what they were worried about. We really did have a very innocent upbringing. My parents never explained the 'facts of life' to me and neither did the school. During a recent conversation with another 'old boy' of the school I discovered that a boy whom I thought had left the school of his own free will was, in fact, expelled for interfering with another pupil.

I have always been proud of the school, and its achievements. I am a member of the Old Boys' Association and I attended many of the Old Boys' Dinners. I was the first old boy to become a governor of the school and I left the Board as the first 'old boy' Chairman. I met Canon Parsons shortly after my time on the Board and was able to enjoy the very obvious delight he found in this information.

In more recent years my practice has been the architects for the school, and I have enjoyed designing staff accommodation, a sixth form commercial study unit, and a new drama and music centre. I have just completed a new sports pavilion.

My best friend at school was Sean O'Mahony, and when we left we continued to see each other on Saturdays. We would go for a few beers before going on to a dance at the Catholic youth club in Whetstone, or The Royalty, Southgate. We spent most of our time talking about our future. He had not left school to enter a university or follow a career. He left with the specific intention of becoming a millionaire as quickly as possible. He had already decided that the easiest way of achieving this was in the music industry. He tried writing pop music and managing pop groups without any great success, but eventually made his first million by producing the first of the books created for the fans of a pop group. He was lucky enough to sell the idea to The Beatles shortly after they became popular. It was simply called 'The Beatles Book'. Before long he was also employing nine girls to stuff photos of The Beatles into envelopes for the readers of the magazine. The last I heard of him was that he had set up a publishing company.

CHAPTER 4

The Second World War

When war broke out we were on holiday in Eire visiting the many members of father's family in Dublin. There had been a question of cancelling the holiday, but father was convinced there would be no war. However, at the end of the first week he received a telegram recalling him to London. He was still sure the war was not going to happen and insisted that the rest of us finish our holiday.

When, a week later, war was declared, we attempted to return to England. On arrival at the terminal, mother was told that although we could travel to England we would not be allowed to enter on Mother's Irish passport. Eire was sympathetic to Germany and we were technically 'aliens'. It did not take long for our English mother to get an English passport but, by the time we were ready to leave, our home in Harlesden in the North East of London had been bombed. Father sought to purchase another house but was only able to obtain a police flat. By the time he had the flat ready we had been in Ireland eighteen months.

We enjoyed living in the police flat. It was over the Magistrates' Court in Kings Cross Road. We were able to climb over the fire escape onto the lower roofs of the courts and watch proceedings through the roof lights. We were also able to watch the doodle bugs (flying bombs) from the wrought iron fire escape stairs at the back of the property. Many of them went over our area, on their way to other parts of London. They made a very distinctive noise while they were flying towards their target. Then the engine would stop, and there was silence until it hit the ground. The explosion that followed could be heard for miles. Our excitement was gained by trying to guess where each bomb was going to land. The only one frightened was mother who not infrequently caught us and insisted that we came back into the flat.

My only other recollection of the war occurred when Derek and I went with our parents to a wedding in the City. The reception went on till late, and we spent the night in an air raid shelter in the basement of an office block, near the restaurant that had provided the reception. Before we had a chance to sleep, the air raid sirens went off and the noise of falling bombs and anti-aircraft guns became deafening. The intensity made it obvious that we were in a target area, and that the raid was severe. We could hear falling masonry as well as the bombs. The few people in the shelter were becoming frightened and a little panicky, and my policeman father was busy trying to calm everyone down between his visits to assess the situation above ground. This duty he shared with the wardens and other police officers. They were afraid we might be trapped by the fire and eventually decided we would be safer if we left the City. We took to the streets and walked between the array of fire fighters, water pipes and rubble for the short distance to the nearest underground station. On the way we were joined by others trying to escape from the City. I still remember the sound of bombs and gunfire, and the sight of the falling brick and stone brightly lit up by the flames. When we reached the underground station we went down into the tunnels. My father took my hand and we walked between the lines at the head of a growing column of people. What made the walk so memorable was the scene as we came out of the tunnel at Farringdon Road Station. The whole blazing glass roof of this above-ground station came crashing down on the lines in front of us. It looked as if it was raining glass. If we had reached the station a few moments sooner we would have been buried under it. As it was, we were able to wait until the fire brigade removed the glass and the remains of the roof. Then we left Farringdon Road station for our walk to Kings Cross Road and home. It was amazing to find how concentrated the bombing was on the City. By the time we reached Mount Pleasant sorting office we had left any visual sign of the bombing behind us. Only the sounds in the distance remained.

The only holidays we spent in the Kings Cross Road flat were when the folks were unable to find safer accommodation for us. We spent one holiday evacuated to Neath in South Wales. This gave us a little understanding of what being evacuated was like. It really was very different from being with relatives or the friends of our parents. It was more like being at our boarding school. There was no feeling of being loved. Life was based on a series of instructions. We were told to do things that we would have done anyway. The woman we stayed with lived on her own, and was very untidy. All our meals seemed to consist of greens. It was difficult to understand her strong Welsh ascent and she wanted us to go to chapel with her on Sundays. She could not understand why we preferred to go to our church which was further away. She also had the strange habit of referring to her dead husband as if he was up the chimney. We thought that she believed his soul had left his body and gone via the chimney to Paradise. It was only later that we discovered he had been cremated and his ashes were in a jar on the mantelpiece. The only good thing I can remember about the holiday was being able to spend long hours learning to fish in the ponds at the end of the road.

Although our school was only just out of the centre of London at North Finchley, we were unaware of the war during term time, and I have no other memories of the most momentous thing that has happened in my lifetime. I do not even recollect what I was doing on VE (Victory in Europe) day or VJ (Victory over Japan) day. I know that there were a great number of street parties but I do not remember being at any of them. It may be that we were as sheltered by the boarding school from the rejoicing as we were from the devastation.

CHAPTER 5

Becoming an Architect

Some time before I left school my father had reason to stop a man named Scott for a minor traffic offence. In taking his particulars he discovered that he was the principal of the School of Architecture at the Northern Polytechnic. He asked him for advice on my education to become an architect. Scott said it was difficult owing to the reservation of 90 per cent of the places for ex-servicemen, but as I was too young to start in further education I should look for work in an architect's office and he would save me a place in his architectural school the following year. In the meantime I could apply for a position with a practice he was associated with called Hubert Lidbetter & Son. He would have a word with them for me. If I was accepted it would be easier for him to keep in contact with me. The Lidbetters were Quakers, and their practice had won the Gold Medal for the meeting house and offices facing the front of Euston Station. They were also the last firm to be listed as 'Architects to the King'. I therefore thought that I was very lucky to be offered an apprenticeship.

Their offices were at 2, Verulam Buildings in Gray's Inn, and I thoroughly enjoyed travelling into town. I even enjoyed the work, although it was mostly preparing the linen and removing blots for the architectural assistants. Blots were common in those days because drawing pens were made up of two adjustable prongs that ink just flowed out of, especially when one was drawing lines on the shiny waxed linen cloth.

Mr Scott was not a frequent visitor to the office but when he did arrive he was annoyed to find I had been made an apprentice. He declared that it was no longer an acceptable way into the profession, and he became even more determined to find me a place in his school, with the result that I actually started at the Northern Polytechnic that summer, when I was just sixteen.

I had got used to working with older men during my holiday work but sharing a classroom with them as equals was very different and at first very difficult. There were only two other students straight from school and they had stayed on till the end of their 6th forms. The remainder were 'demobbed' from the services and were all over twenty-four. Some were in their thirties and married. Many of them had been in engineering and surveying before the war, and had been allocated similar work in the services, so already had experience in some of the subjects. They were committed to work and not about to enter into the social life of students. It is surprising then that we achieved a happy community. The older members became very fatherly towards us. My best friend, Clem Shepherd, who lived nearby in Muswell Hill, was twenty-four. He had been involved in the D-Day landings as a Lieutenant in the Royal Navy.

I did very well in art and design, but was finding it difficult to concentrate on the written subjects. I failed the exams at the end of the first, second and third years, so was asked to leave. It was at about this time that I was diagnosed with dyslexia. Although this condition probably did make studying difficult for me, was not the main reason for my failure. I just had not worked hard enough.

Mother was as close to angry as I had ever seen her, but it was not clear as to whether it was with me or the polytechnic. She hunted around, looking for advice from anyone she knew, and was introduced by our doctor to the administrator of the Architectural Association School of Architecture. She arranged an appointment for me to meet him with a portfolio of my work. I was at the time spending the holiday earning good money in a Norfolk Farm Camp and was not anxious to leave, but mother came up to make sure I agreed to go.

At the interview, the administrator told me that they had nearly 100 applicants for the three places available for the third year but he was able to say from my portfolio that I would stand a good chance the following year. Two weeks later he phoned to say that one of the successful applicants had dropped out and as they had not made arrangements for a replacement I could have the place. I have a feeling that being thrown out of a less prestigious school for reasons other than poor design had something to do with it. A few years after I had finished at the 'AA' the great architect Richard Rogers was accepted there with serious dyslexia, and developed very well before leaving to get a doctorate at Yale. I have since learnt that the condition is not uncommon in the profession.

The Architectural Association was good for me. They concentrated on design and allowed us to take books into exams. They considered that being able to use information was more important than being able to remember it. We were also able to work in groups, and to do the work anywhere we wanted to. We tended to go into the main school only for lectures and our studio for meetings and the 'Crits'. These were criticisms of our work by staff or staff and students. Marks were not considered appropriate. I thrived on this form of education and might have received an honours diploma if I had not caught pleurisy while producing my final thesis. I managed to get my concept down on paper, but the presentation suffered from the limited time I was able to devote to it.

I still had to pass an examination in architectural practice. This has to follow a minimum period of a year in an architectural office. Private practice offices were only just getting established after the war and architects were not keen to take students without office experience. The Greater London Council, or the Ministry of Works were the best options. The Greater London Council was my preferred choice. I made an application and was short listed. When, on the appointed day, I arrived at County Hall I was shocked to see the size of my competition, but I thought that the prestige of my school and the quality of the work in my portfolio would secure me a place. When I was called into the interview an assistant took my portfolio and placed it in front of the first of some eight panellists. The chairman asked me some very secular questions and I was aware of my drawings being passed so quickly from one panellist to the next that no form of assessment could have been taking place. I became angry and when they asked me to collect my drawings quickly from where they had ended up I told them that the portfolio was intact when I came into the room and I was entitled to receive it in the same condition before I left. They returned the portfolio intact but I did not get the job.

When I had my interview at the Ministry of Works I went with a different attitude and got the job. There were about eight of us, newly qualified architects, starting that September, and we became a community which made the boring life tolerable. We found being used as draughtsmen, adapting 'in house' standard details and schedules under unqualified people very difficult. The head of our section had never studied architecture but had gained his position during the war when many architects had joined the services. We saw the Ministry as a stop gap. Private practice was what we were aiming for. One of the ways to escape the boredom was to put in for promotion, or to answer requests for site survey work. I did, rather arrogantly, put in for promotion after about six months, but I was considered to have insufficient experience. I also acted as a surveying assistant for a while in Scotland. But by far my most exciting time was when I went to Aldermaston.

I had answered a request from the site architect's office for a model maker, and, as temporary staff accommodation was available, I went. I was briefed by the site architect to make a model of the existing typical 1950s utilitarian office building that stood at the end of the drive from the main entrance. I was then to make models of three different ways of disguising the water tank prepared by senior architects in London. This would enable the minister, on his next visit, to see whether any of the designs would overcome the criticism he had expressed on a previous visit. I was given part of a hut, access to a Land Rover, a petty cash facility to purchase materials, and permission to do as much overtime as was necessary to get the model finished before the Minister's next visit.

When the Minister appeared I was present to put the disguises in place. After this part of the meeting was over Sir William Penney, the Director of Aldermaston, approached me to discuss the possibility of setting up a unit of model makers. He would find research people from his side who could make models of what went into the buildings and I would then encase them to give "those people in London a better idea of what we want."

The following day I was joined by two engineering model makers with a brief for our first building. They were very good and the equipment they brought enabled us to produce better models. Parts of the model of their plant moved and we had lighting. The unit lasted long enough for us to get our first model to London and then we were wound up. I never discovered why. It could have been the degree of overtime, or the money we were spending on materials, or that we had nobody of rank in charge. It might, just possibly, have been the fact that a draughtsman was playing such a large part in the design process.

Shortly after I returned from Aldermaston I passed my Professional Practice examination, and was offered a position as Architectural Assistant with a private firm of architects. When I submitted my notice to the Ministry I was asked to give my reasons for leaving. I decided not to give any. This led to a series of visits to people of ascending rank, each of whom tried to get an answer from me. It occurred to me early on in the process that if I said I was only prepared to tell the Chief Architect I might just manage to achieve it. I really did believe that I was on a mission to help correct the way newly qualified architects were being treated. Finally, I got an interview with the Chief Architect. I showed him the advertisement for qualified architects which painted a very different picture from the one I was leaving and said I felt that I owed it to the profession to bring it to his attention. His name was on the advertisement and he could do something about it. He was very angry and treated me like a naughty school boy. What hurt me most was his opinion that I had wasted his time. Within a very few minutes I was told to get out of his office.

I went back some years later to see the colleagues I had started with and, with the exception of the lad from Liverpool, who had managed to get a job before me, they were all still there. Their main reason for staying was the security and the pension. Some of them had managed to get on the promotion ladder. I was very pleased, however, that I had left when I did. Otherwise I might, like them, have got to enjoy the security of a job for life.

CHAPTER 6

Working holidays

I spent most of my student holidays topping up the pocket money my parents were able to give me. One Christmas I delivered parcel post from the back of a van and another I worked as a filing clerk for the Inland Revenue, but most of the winter holidays were spent in hotel kitchens washing up. Most of the summer holidays I worked in the fresh air. One year I was employed as a Red Coat at Butlins. It was a fun job. I was Vice-Captain for organised games during the day, while at night I was on ballroom duty. This meant spending the whole evening dancing with the least popular girls. We were not allowed to choose a partner until a specified time after the start of each dance, though we did manage to cheat a little. A girl one was interested in could be persuaded to refuse partners until the specified time had elapsed. I would have worked at Butlins for all my summer holidays if we had not had to commit to working for the whole season. The polytechnic would not have found that acceptable.

Most of my summer holidays were spent with my friend, Clem Shepherd, at what were called Farm Camps. The ones we went to were ex-army or prisoner-of-war camps in counties bordering London. They consisted of Nissen huts made of corrugated iron sheets on semi-circular frames. They were long enough to take about ten beds and wide enough to accommodate a bed on either side of a generous aisle. The only upright walls were at the back and front of the buildings. Hanging anything up was impossible.

We paid thirty-two shillings and six pence (£1.75) for a week's board and lodging, and one could earn ten shillings (50p) a day picking fruit or putting the fruit into cans. It attracted mostly students, coal miners, and people in the catering trade. If the weather was good we could earn enough for evening beers in the village pub, and still save enough for a cheap holiday.

Most of the work was boring, but it gave us the opportunity to think about life and our careers. It also helped us to appreciate the advantage we had of working for a degree. Perhaps, most of all, it helped us to look forward to the holiday the work was making possible. Some of those holidays were very memorable. I particularly recall my first trip to Europe. I had not realised it would be so different. Restaurants and cafés were popular long before they became common in England. The food was different and better in those days. Everyone lived in flats, and every block of flats had a concierge. People went to work in smart clothes, wine was cheap and beer was almost non-existent.

One summer, we left the camp to hitch-hike to the Edinburgh Festival, and almost immediately stopped an American airman from the local base, who asked us where we were going. When we told him, he wanted to know more about the Festival; he liked the idea and decided it would be an ideal place to spend his leave. He said that he would take us. We got into the back of his comfortable American car and didn't stop until we reached Edinburgh Castle. He was keen to visit the castle so we wished each other a good holiday and that was the last we saw of him. We felt a bit guilty about convincing him to drive so far, especially as we had given him no idea of the distance involved. I know now, however, that Americans are quite used to long drives across the USA, and he probably was not as put out as we feared.

The last time I went to one of these camps I booked in for two weeks with the intention of extending my stay if I liked it there. I did, and the work was plentiful. I approached the ex-army warden and asked him for an extension. He said he was unhappy with his deputy warden and if I would take his job I could stay, but I felt I could not do that so my extension was left in abeyance.

The deputy warden was a medical student who considered his pleasure more important than his duties. Nevertheless, he was a likeable person and very popular. Towards the end of my second week, however, the police came to arrest him for non-payment of alimony and something dishonest involving shopkeepers in the village. As we all turned out to wave him goodbye the warden asked me again if I would take his job. Of course I said 'yes' and the job was mine. I am not sure he understood why my answer had changed.

I was paid more than a farm worker. My basic wage was £5 a week and if I decided to work with the campers, I could act as foreman for which I would receive ten shillings more than the campers. I was later to get a Ministry of Agriculture and Fisheries driving licence. This entitled me to an additional £2 a week for driving the campers to work, and extra money if I drove the tractor or other mechanical appliances on the farms. My living conditions also improved. I stopped sharing a Nissen hut with twenty other campers and moved into one all to myself.

My main responsibility was taking the work requests phoned into the warden and allocating them among sixty and seventy campers. I had then to see that the work was properly carried out. As the tasks varied in difficulty, and people were anxious to choose with whom they worked, I was the recipient of much Guinness when I took them to the local pub in the evening. I was also well looked after by the landlords of the pubs I chose to take them to.

One of these was frequented by a gipsy family. The father was very concerned that his two rather attractive young daughters should not fall foul of some of our young lads. He tended to stand propping up one end of the mantel over the fireplace on the wall adjacent to the bar. From here he could see all that was going on and be seen to be in charge of affairs. It therefore seemed appropriate for me to prop up the other end. This situation tended to create a challenge for our young lads, which his young girls appeared to enjoy. It became a feature of our evenings, especially as I encouraged it by giving him some of my surplus pints. Our conversation was limited and tended to flow from questions I asked about his life. I have a strong memory of him illustrating a story about poaching by taking out of an inside overcoat pocket his pet ferret, an attractive little thing and very well behaved. I hadn't known the creature was there.

One part of my role, however, I had not foreseen, nor been told about: I was to replace the chef on his day off. My only experience of cooking was what I had gained camping with the scouts. I had an Italian ex-prisoner of war and his wife as kitchen hands. They carried out the worst of the work. She prepared the vegetables and did the washing up; he fed the stoves with coal and did the washing up. I had to prepare the packed lunches, and cook the breakfast and dinner for about sixty hungry people. I was on my own and the cooking appliance was a solid fuel range. But the chef trained me well and I eventually came to enjoy the challenge.

The chef was an ex-army cook who had spent most of

his time in India. From him I was able to learn both standard English cooking and Indian cuisine, and I have many good reasons to be thankful for what he taught me. I learnt many tricks of the trade. I also learnt a few tricks which I am pleased to say I have never made use of. Putting a piece of soda in the teapot bleaches the leaves pure white and makes the tea go at least twice as far. Putting salt in coffee achieves the same effect. Beating oil into butter and margarine makes them go further. Today this has become respectable and the result is called 'spreadable butter'. There were others you would prefer not to hear about.

This summer was the one immediately after I had been asked to leave the Northern Polytechnic.

CHAPTER 7

Gooday & Noble

My experience at the Ministry of Works did not cause me to question my choice of career. I was still confident that private practice would be different, and I was lucky to be accepted by Gooday & Noble who had an office at 2, Cadogan Place, just off Sloane Street. They were a comparatively new partnership of two architects created to design some of the infrastructure for the 1951 Festival of Britain. This provided them with the publicity which brought interesting work into the practice. It could have led to a great future for them but by the time I joined they were having difficulties in working with each other. As senior assistant to Wycliffe Noble one of my duties was to represent his views to his partner. The other senior assistant was Ronald Gillings who acted in the same capacity for Leslie Gooday. Ronald was to become my partner when I started my own practice, and the roles we played for this practice proved to be invaluable training for running our later partnership.

Wycliffe was a member of the Salvation Army and the drummer in their famous religious pop group, The Joystrings. He was instrumental in creating their success in records like 'It's an open secret', and 'On a starry night'. He gave me my first opportunity to work on a religious building: the Salvation

Hall in Hendon, which has since been demolished to make way for shops. I did the working drawings from the original design and supervised the building on site.

The second project I worked on was for Technicolor Limited, who had offices almost opposite the entrance to Heathrow Airport on the Bath Road. It was an American company which controlled the whole of the process of producing coloured film. In those days if you wanted your film to be in technicolor it was their cameramen who took the film, their staff who processed the it, made the copies and stored the originals. This was to protect their copyright from the other companies competing for the colour market. If the film was made in England, all these processes were carried out from the buildings on the Bath Road.

I had produced some of the drawings and saw the completion of the dining room, and the beginnings of the fireproof, insect proof, and earthquake proof film storage building. The dining room would have been called a canteen in an English company but then it would not have been like a restaurant with well designed chairs and tables, and first class food. It was here that I found that Americans tend to start their meals with a salad, and I got to like the idea.

Wycliffe was, as indeed I was to become, an office architect. He was not keen on spending his time on the sites supervising the work. It therefore fell to me to take on most of the site work for the Salvation Army Hall, and all of the site work for Technicolor Ltd. This entitled me to take the office car, Wycliffe's 1922 Bentley, a superb beast that could reach speeds of sixty miles an hour between the traffic lights on the Bath Road, but needed longer than the warning yellow light to stop it.

There was a time when it was felt important for me to be available on site for most of the week. This left me with leisure to spend in the room where the film copies were examined for faults. The operator had full control of the speed and direction of the film. I particularly enjoyed the few occasions I was able to use the controls myself. We take these functions for granted now but at that time the ability to control something one could not normally control was exciting.

I would also receive an occasional ticket from those given to the office for film previews in the Technicolor theatre. These were held for the stars and makers of the films to see their finished product before it was released to the cinema chains. The theatre held about fifty people seated in comfortable chairs with adjoining tables for the buffet. These opportunities to see films before they were released provided me with good party conversation.

It was while I was with Gooday & Noble that I decided to start my own practice; I was learning to see the people I met as potential clients. With this attitude of mind I persuaded a young builder to develop a site he thought would be suitable for housing in the centre of Findon, a village five miles from the coast at Worthing. He was short of the money required to do the development, so I offered my services in exchange for one of the cottages. I assured him that I would be able to find him a loan facility when I had obtained planning consent. He agreed and I obtained the planning consent and finance for ten cottages. This provided father with a retirement home and myself with a weekend retreat. I think he must have felt that he paid too much for my services, however, because he never came back.

CHAPTER 8

The Chef

The knowledge I had gained cooking on the old solid fuel range at the farm camp gave me an idea for improving my evening work in hotel kitchens. I persuaded a friend from school, Reg Conrad, now the assistant manager of The Rubens Hotel, to get me indentured as an apprentice chef. This improved both my chance of getting work and the type of work I was getting. I was now preparing vegetables instead of washing up.

This change in my work coincided with my starting at the Architectural Association where the allocation of study time was more within my control and I was able to spend a little more of it earning money. I was helped by the fact that people in catering move from job to job quite frequently. Disappearing occasionally to finish school work was not a problem. I just changed hotel.

After a while I became interested in what we were cooking and started to achieve some knowledge and skills. I was given more responsible work and eventually promoted to the patisserie department. I became good at the artistic side of the business and spent much time with the piping bag. I also became skilled at butter- and ice-sculpture, something I was called upon to do after I had left college and was working for my professional practice examination.

When I was fully qualified and employed by Gooday & Noble I spent some time with their Interior Design consultant, Terence Conran, who was working on the interior designs at Technicolor Ltd with us. He was then planning to open a coffee bar at the Knightsbridge end of Sloane Street. He saw it as a shop window for displaying his furniture and it occurred to me that a similar venture might conceivably attract an architectural client. It would have the added advantage of providing capital to start a practice. I was anxious to begin on my own, even if it meant freelancing for other architects, and was already spending my evenings producing working drawings for a school in Africa – a commission (my first) for an architect in Hampstead.

It was whilst working for this architect that I found a small workman's café on the first floor over garages in Elizabeth Mews, for sale at a very low price. It was behind the shops on the north side of England's Lane in Hampstead. The customers were chauffeurs from the car hire company that owned many of the garages. The demand for this form of hire had declined, however, and the café was no longer a viable proposition. I persuaded my friend Reg to leave his job at The Rubens and join me in starting a coffee bar in these premises. He would work full time on the conversion, and I would help him in the evenings and weekends, retaining my architectural job for as long as we needed the income to pay for the work.

We formed Murcon Restaurants Ltd, and borrowed money from banks, families, and friends to purchase the lease. The conversion was completed in a couple of months, its design based on a great deal of bench seating, low lighting, things to do with boats, and an enormous Pavoni coffee machine. We called the place 'The Loft' and spent a great deal of time in discussing how we could make it successful with no passing trade. We realised we needed a gimmick and decided to produce a main course for two shillings and sixpence (25p) that was filling and, crucially, less expensive than anywhere else in the area. We offered spaghetti or risotto, and used the same form of Bolognese sauce for both, but nobody seemed to notice. The rest of the menu was based on the grill. Customers could have almost anything as long as it was grilled and served with chips, a practice that enabled us to produce food very quickly and in little space. Reg or I were able to handle all the cooking, even on very busy weekends.

Our gimmick worked. The students appreciated the opportunity to fill up for very little money, and were soon turning up in sufficient numbers for us to make a profit. The Pavoni was a great help. I never could understand how, having watched their pennies while choosing the food, they would happily pay an exorbitant price for coffee. We also did well with the grills, which were preferred when the students came in pairs on the weekends with their own bottles of wine.

Another idea we had which proved attractive was, on Saturdays only, to allow customers from other lands to earn a meal for themselves and a partner if they were prepared to spend the morning teaching us how to prepare one of their country's dishes, which would then become the special for that evening. It was popular and we learnt a lot by doing it.

We wore dark green polo neck jumpers, black trousers and black cummerbunds. We never employed people to entertain but there were very few evenings when somebody did not sing or play an instrument. Many of those who played for us became famous, among them Lonnie Donegan, Dill Jones, Acker Bilk, and regulars Robin Hall and Jimmy McGregor.

The customers became a community, celebrating their birthdays, weddings and other special events in the coffee bar. We kept several old cars to enable staff to get home at night. We also used these vehicles to take the customers, and food unsold at the end of the evening, to one of the swimming pools on Hampstead Heath. Here there would be singing, dancing, and swimming. Indeed, this was where I learnt to swim.

Although The Loft was situated in a residential area we gained considerable support from our neighbours. When a few of them objected to our presence the majority of the neighbouring owners of the shops and houses joined the police in giving evidence in our favour at the local Magistrates' Court. The case was dismissed.

It had been difficult enough to work in the office by day and the coffee bar at night but as we became more successful and the customers wanted us to stay open into the early hours of the morning it became impossible for me to maintain my day job. I had to give up working for Gooday & Noble. What little time I could take off from The Loft was used to start my practice.

After two years we found our second site, a wet fish shop and basement in Belsize Village. The design included a large cauldron at the entrance in which we kept the soup of the day. We called this coffee bar 'The Witch's Cauldron' and specialised in serving a better quality of food in a larger kitchen than we had at The Loft. By this time we were in the 'swinging sixties' and people wanted more exciting dishes from a greater range of countries. Grills, with the exception of steak, were out and even steak was taking a new form: steak au poivre and chateau-briand, the latter shared between two, were becoming popular. Chicken Kiev was giving way to boeuf bourguignon and boeuf Stroganoff. Liebfraumilch and Mateus Rosé were out and Nuits St George and Châteauneuf-du-Pape were in.

Reg ran The Witch's Cauldron and I stayed with The Loft until the architectural practice became more successful. We then employed Rons to manage The Loft. He was a charming, good-looking Scotsman who was very popular with the customers, but a poor manager. The place soon began to look run down and many of our regular customers moved to The Witch's Cauldron, so we closed it.

The Cauldron went from strength to strength and I converted the basement into a coffee bar, leaving the ground floor as a restaurant. A few years later we had the chance to purchase the adjoining shop and basement and were able, by phasing the programme, to convert the ground floor of the new unit into a first class restaurant, with a coffee bar next door on the ground floor of the original unit; the basement of the two units became a licensed coffee bar. The price of all the food was still kept very low and meals were within what young people on dates could afford, provided they did not take too much advantage of the well priced alcohol.

Long before the final stage of the business had been achieved Reg married Daphne, a charming and vivacious girl from Northern Ireland, who was a great success with the clientele of the basement coffee bar. She presided over a table for about eight people reserved just for the owners and their guests. Wine for this table was normally on the house. Regular customers would vie with each other to be invited to sit there. Reg and Daphne spent all their time in this very 'hands on' form of business which put great stress on their marriage. Eventually, Reg left to join Lew Hoad in creating a tennis village on the Costa del Sol. A man called Joel then became the manager and subsequently married Daphne. They left the country some time later to escape taxation and created a very successful bar called 'Daffers' on Ibiza. The Witch's Cauldron was closed.

One of The Loft customers was John Evans who had been at the Architectural Association School of Architecture; we became close friends. I frequently took a break at his house in an adjoining road, or at the Belsize and Hampstead Tennis

Club which was owned and run by his parents. I also spent time at the Martello tower his father was converting into an hotel down on the coast. One day John's father asked me to coach his son in getting his qualification. I did try, but he was more interested in becoming a property developer and converting the tower.

When I stopped working in the coffee bar John and I would meet for drinks on Friday evenings. By then, the bar had ceased to appeal, and there did not appear to be an acceptable alternative. We considered various ideas and ultimately settled on taking over one of the many old sports club venues that were unused on Saturday and Sunday evenings and might welcome a little extra income by having their premises turned into a temporary restaurant. The London Rowing Club expressed interest and was prepared to let us use their beautiful 1850s timber venue at Putney Bridge.

With the help of John's brother, Peter Evans, who had owned and run The Cat's Whisker and was now the owner of the London Steak Houses, we furnished the Rowing Club. A pantechnicon full of furniture, crockery and linen would arrive after the last rower had left the changing room on the Saturday. We would then rearrange and furnish the club house, take stock of the bar, and start preparing the food for an eight o'clock opening. The same thing had to happen in reverse on Sunday: everything had to be cleared and loaded onto the pantechnicon before we went home.

The food comprised cold meats and fish, patés, and a large variety of different salads, well prepared but not expensive. It was on the alcohol that we hoped to make a small profit. The entertainment was a steel band, augmented by a variety of solo artists. Steel bands were all the rage at that time but we had a great deal of trouble with them. We were never sure when they would arrive or how many musicians would turn up, so we set up a steel band management company which gave us a little more control.

We had seen it as something we could enjoy with our friends but it did not take long to discover that nobody has enough friends on which to base a business. After a very slow start, however, our enterprise became known and popular, and we began to make good money out of enjoying ourselves with our friends. We had solved our problem – until the government brought in legislation governing the amount of alcohol one could drink if one were driving. When the Act came in everyone took it very seriously. They would not drink at all if they were going to drive and, in consequence, our numbers dropped below what we needed to cover our costs. Hoping things would improve when people became more used to it, we carried on for a while, but having to give up drinking ourselves was what finally caused us to relinquish the enterprise.

Nevertheless, we still thought our ideas were good and started to look for a similar venue nearer home. We could not find a sports club but we did discover a pub in Islington called The Island Queen with a large public room on the first floor. In the beginning it was going to be the same kind of arrangement as at the Rowing Club, using only the first floor and letting out the ground floor to someone else, but this proved impossible because of the licence. We would have to take responsibility for the whole premises. We were about to give up the idea when John's father died and John decided that the pub would fit his new domestic circumstances. He took over the licence and created a very successful venue, famous for the life-sized figures of people which hung from the ceiling, It had a good restaurant on the first floor, run by my friend Leon Manzi, while the flat on the top floor provided John with an office and a home he could share with his recently widowed mother.

John went on to open a chain of pubs in the Ipswich area, later going into semi-retirement at a country inn in Cuckfield, where I was often called upon to cook for New Year's Eve dinners or open air barbecues in the summer. He subsequently gave this up and, with my help, converted the Grand Hotel in Frinton into a residential home for the elderly. Then, feeling he was finally ready, he retired to New Zealand.

The Rowing Club was my last proper attempt at catering. I still miss the life and it has not been difficult for restaurant owners to persuade me to help out, cooking Spanish food on a wood burning range in a restaurant in Hampstead or Italian food on a normal catering range in the San Carlo, next to my home in Highgate. I also enjoy cooking for parties at our flat. We have a Winter Solstice party for some forty or fifty guests and I cooked for eighty people at my mother's eightieth birthday party and ninety at her ninetieth birthday party.

CHAPTER 9

Ann

I can no longer remember the first time I met my first serious girlfriend, but the second occasion is a vivid memory. I was in my early twenties and it was at a twenty-first birthday party, held on a mink farm somewhere in the country. The centre point of the party was a Victorian open sided bandstand. A small group was playing and guests were dancing. Other guests were rowing on the river which flowed through the estate. Yet others were enjoying the buffet in the grand house while the rest were to be found in chattering groups scattered around the spacious woods that housed the mink farm. I had arrived late and was doing a tour of the party, hoping to find friends I expected to be there, when I bumped into a girl whom seemed rather special. I thought I had seen her before. She was tall, with excellent posture, not exactly pretty but her features were perfect. We talked and I became oblivious of almost everything else. I can remember dancing in the bandstand and ending the evening sitting on cushions in the main house. She left the party with the friends who had brought her and I stayed on in the house. Before we parted I said I would give her a call. She replied: "That's what you said last time." I was quite taken aback. I certainly could not remember any more than feeling I had seen her before.

All I could do was to reassure her that this time it would be different – and it was.

I could not get Ann out of my mind and made contact the following day. I then spent as much time in her company as I could get away from the practice. We not only enjoyed each other's company, we enjoyed each other's friends, and I developed an enthusiasm for Ann's major hobby: motor sport and motor cars. She had not started work and was restoring two old Lagondas, which we entered for vintage car rallies. (We also entered rallies for modern cars.) Her father was an executive director at Ford so we were able to use the cars the engineers prepared for their official rally team – Consuls, Zephyrs and Zodiacs, but mostly Consuls. In those days there was no dearth of amateur rallies, mostly illegal, and we were members of a club that told us by mail when and where the rallies would take place. There were three basic types. The first two were excuses for racing on country roads. With the first, we would be given the route and speed of a vehicle leaving a particular place at a particular time. We would have to get a card signed by the driver of that vehicle as he crossed the course we were given. The second consisted of collecting several specific items from particular places on or near the route we had been given. In both cases, the first to complete the route with tasks achieved was the winner of a small trifle. The routes were well manned with voluntary marshals who would cancel the rally if the police discovered it. The speeds we had to achieve to win were virtually as fast as the cars would go. These races took place on normal roads with weekend traffic. There were not so many cars on the roads in those days but, with hindsight, I can appreciate that they were very dangerous. I remember an occasion when we became aware of smoke coming from the back seat of the car: it was alight. Probably, the lighted tip of one of our cigarettes had been blown there. I had to climb into the back to put the fire out while Ann continued to pass a line of traffic on a three lane highway. She was driving at maximum speed in order to catch the car we had to stop for a signature. I did put the fire out, we did catch the car – and we won a cigarette lighter for coming third.

The third type of rally was not illegal and not at all frightening. It consisted of driving backwards and forwards on a very difficult course between cones set out in a car park or playground. Penalty points were given each time you hit a cone. Ann, as our number one driver, would spend hours practising this type of driving and the many other necessary skills, like changing tyres and other components that had shorter lives in those days. I was merely the navigator and did not take my role as seriously.

You must not think we spent all our time together driving. We also went to the cinema, parties, and to my mother's on Sundays for lunch. I had never introduced a girl friend to mother before because I was afraid she would either push me into marriage or decide the girl was not good enough for her son. In fact, my mother liked her and was only anxious lest I make a hasty decision.

Ann did not get on well with her parents. I don't think they were happy with her not having a real job. Repairing old motor cars did not score very highly as an occupation with them. Ann lived in her own flat in Kensington a long way from the parental home. I never met her mother but I did encounter her father a few times when he was working in London. He was extremely conservative in outlook. On one occasion he asked Ann to organise a dinner in "one of those new 'with it' places" where he could entertain an important young business man and his girlfriend. Our reward was to help him entertain them. He felt that The Savoy, his usual venue for business entertaining, would not have been suitable for these young people. We chose a very 'with it' restaurant in Beauchamp Place off the Brompton Road. When he arrived with his guests we were already ensconced having a drink. He was irritable and apologised to his guests for our choice of restaurant. It was smaller than he was used to and obviously not smart enough. The waiter came for our drinks order. When he got to Ann's father he was told that he did not want "just a small whisky but a proper drink". He also wanted to put the water in himself. The waiter, sensing the situation, explained that they served water and ice separately, and the measure they used was what he believed was called a treble. He hoped that would be suitable. The drinks came and Ann's father asked for the menu, only to be told that they did not have menus. The waiter not only described the dishes being served that evening, but went into great detail as to how the chef had prepared the ingredients that morning. I think the episode with the drink made her father more careful and he accepted the absence of a menu. The meal was, as usual, excellent. His guests were obviously very happy with the restaurant and I felt that her father's discomfort probably added to their enjoyment.

My friendship with Ann ended abruptly, alas. She told me on the telephone that my friend, Reg Conrad, had taken her out and she felt it only fair to tell me that she was very attracted to him. Our relationship should become Platonic, she felt. There followed the worst few days of my life. I now knew that I was in love. I had fallen in love with her without realising it. I missed her immediately and at every moment. I could not forget her and kept reliving the times we had spent together. I thought I would never get over it. The fact that I had lost her to a friend made it worse. Now that Reg was running The Witch's Cauldron, however, I did not have to see him or her. The physical pain faded, however, as I concentrated on the practice and eventually I worked my way out of love. Her relationship with Reg did not last long but, having got over losing her, I never wanted to rekindle so intense a feeling with Ann again.

The next time I saw her was at a party where she introduced me to the man to whom she was engaged. I got an invitation to the wedding and we did see each other occasionally afterwards as we still had some friends in common. Her marriage did not last long and we finally ended up being just good friends. I always invited her to our Christmas party.

I do not think I ever fell in love again – certainly not with the same intensity that I had loved Ann. Ann was the only one who succeeded in competing with the attraction of a new commission.

There were other times when I was not involved in producing designs. Times when I would want to relax in the evenings. I would go to the theatre, cinema, or to have dinner out. These occasions were always more enjoyable with female company. I know that the longer I went without female company the more I wanted it. I therefore cultivated a number of women friends who would accept an invitation. Working through my drawer of photographs today, I see them again and I am surprised at how many I can remember and how important a part of my life they became.

Sadly, the last I heard of Ann was that she had died of cancer.

CHAPTER 10

Bernard Vorhaus

My first commission of ten houses was followed by a small warehouse to provide storage for a Spanish furnishings shop in Chelsea. They were interesting projects but not a sufficient basis on which to start a practise. It took the continuity of the work Bernard Vorhaus was offering to do that.

Bernard Vorhaus had left Russia in the early 1920s for the USA, where he became a silent film maker. He subsequently became a director of the early 'talkies'. After the Second World War he came to Europe and was directing a film in Italy when Senator McCarthy started convincing America that communists were a danger to their society. Bernard was a communist and, fearing he might be called to appear before one of the McCarthy 'Witch Hunt' trials, he decided not to return to the States when the film was finished but to look for film work in England. This proved impossible, presumably because it was thought his name on a film would limit its sale in America.

Having to find another means of making a living, Bernard decided to use his savings in the area of property development. He was inspecting property in the Primrose Hill area of Hampstead one afternoon when he sought a cup of tea at the chauffeur's restaurant in Primrose Mews and found that it had become The Loft coffee bar. He came in for a coffee and told us he was very impressed with the theatrical use of lobster pots and other items of fishing tackle with which we had created the new environment. I think he was actually more interested in how cheaply we had achieved the conversion from workman's café to stylish coffee bar. He asked who the designer was and I was able to tell him that it was I, the chef, waiter and washer-up until I could get my architectural practice started. It was the slack period in the middle of the afternoon and we had time to talk. He told me about his career and his property development, and I told him about my work as an architect. This was the beginning of my practice. Bernard was buying large houses in the area and converting them into flats, and he came to the conclusion that his flats might be better if he used my services.

We became good friends and completed many interesting conversions together. Among them was the house in Elsworthy Terrace where Lenin had stayed as a student, and a house in Elsworthy Road where the Duke of Windsor is supposed to have met Mrs Simpson at a cocktail party. A friend of mine from school, Claud Luzzatto, who had the top floor flat in this property, told me the story of the elderly woman living below him who proudly boasted of never having to use her central heating. She would say that she lived in a very warm house, and refused to accept that she was being heated by the flats immediately above and below her.

One morning when we were inspecting properties for development, Bernard asked me to visit a house in the area behind the building, which at that time was the Black Cat cigarette factory in Mornington Crescent, to give advice to the owners. When we arrived they took us up to the top floor inside a mansard roof. There was no furniture and no decoration other than a couple of coats of white emulsion.

On one of the walls, however, there was a drawing of a flying dove with an olive branch in its mouth that I recognised as the Dove of Peace. They explained that it was the original design sketched there by Picasso at an early meeting of CND. They wanted to know if there was any way they could get it off the wall. I explained how difficult it would be, and suggested they contact a professional restorer at one of our national art galleries. Every time I see a copy of the emblem I wonder what happened to the original.

In 1960 when relations with the Soviet Union improved, representation of our two countries was taken to full embassy status and the Russians required housing for the considerable increase in staff that followed. What they wanted were several very large houses converted into self-contained flats with additional communal facilities. The area they favoured was Holland Park because it was possessed of large enough houses which were also fairly close to the existing embassy building.

They advertised for a developer to provide the accommodation; Bernard won the contract, and I became the architect. Because they required the flats as quickly as possible it was decided to enter into contracts with the builders based on three eight-hour shifts per day, six days a week. This increased the costs but enabled us to receive our fees more frequently.

The construction of the flats was uneventful, but working with the embassy staff in the late '60s led to some interesting situations. We were not as accustomed to dealing with people from other lands as we are today. There was very little immigration and no cheap flights abroad. Thomas Cook was still virtually the only travel agent in town.

In practice our client was either the First Secretary or the Chargé d'Affaires. There was no delegation; their office was in the main embassy building in Kensington Palace Gardens.

The front hall contained the telephone exchange as well as the reception, and this formed the security control for the embassy. If your name was on the list of the person you wanted to see you were allowed in. If you were not on the list you would not be seen by anybody. Similarly, if your name was not on the list of the person you wanted to telephone you would not be put through.

All the embassy staff had to use 'pool' cars with a chauffeur and escort. The escorts always wore very long overcoats, I suppose in an attempt to hide the weapons which I assumed they carried. On one very hot day we were driving up Holland Park when our client asked whether we would like to join him for tea. We agreed and he took us to a French patisserie where he ordered tea and pastries with a perfect French accent while we all sat feeling very conspicuous. We should not have been surprised that his accent was so good, however, because all the senior staff at the embassy spoke most European languages perfectly.

The Russians were sensitive about their position in London and some problems which would not usually have seemed out of the ordinary led to the Foreign Office being called to investigate. The most extreme example occurred during the six months' maintenance check on one of the houses. A new boiler exploded and our clients were convinced it was sabotage. They called a meeting with a Foreign Office representative and ourselves. I brought along two representatives from the boiler manufacturer, one of whom had gained his experience making the early cast iron boilers. He was a large, strong man with a peaked cap and a paunch, presumably created by imbibing the beer provided for those working close to the furnace.

He took only a few minutes to inspect the boiler before calling to me in loud cockney, "The cause of the trouble is obvious, guv. The buggers haven't maintained it."

He spoke with such authority that his statement was accepted without argument. The First Secretary simply asked us to get it replaced, and invited us all back to the Embassy for refreshment. This took the form of tea served from an ornate samovar, brought into one of the impressive reception rooms. The boiler expert, now being treated as the guest of honour, was offered the first cup of tea, and was just as blunt in telling our hosts what he thought of it. He said that he had drunk what he thought was the strongest tea on building sites, but this took the biscuit and it did not even have the advantage of being weakened with milk. But he became quite effusive about the quality of the Armenian brandy that followed. He thought it gave 'tea-time' a whole new meaning.

Most of the formal meetings with our clients concluded with a bottle of some superb alcohol, which one consumed in small glasses in one gulp. This custom caused Bernard to be apprehensive about one of the meetings I had arranged for signing a contract. It was early on a Saturday morning. I picked Bernard up in my car and he asked me to support his objection to having a bottle to mark the signing of the contract, explaining that he had a stomach ulcer and had had no breakfast. He was quite sure that any amount of alcohol at that time of day would do him untold damage. I said I would do what I could, but I was not very optimistic.

After the documents were signed the inevitable offer of a glass of vodka was made. Bernard made his plea to be excused. I backed him up as best I could, but both officers present declared that the toast was important for the success of the contract. They did, however, agree to call for only half a bottle. While we were waiting Bernard continued his protest, so one of the officers said that he would order some caviar, because if one ate really first grade caviar on a dry biscuit with each glass of vodka it would counteract the effects of the spirit. The vodka was served and Bernard appeared convinced, probably because it had become clear that they were not going to take 'no' for an answer. After we had finished we took our leave and were escorted to the front door. As soon as we took a breath of the fresh air Bernard became queasy and fell down the steps onto the pavement. One of the officers ran to help him while the other called an ambulance. Bernard came round almost immediately, however, and showed no signs of injury but the officers insisted we wait for the ambulance. Happily, when it arrived the medics gave him a clean bill of health and we were able to leave.

There was an occasion in April 1961, however, when we were detained at the embassy for much longer. Bernard and I had arrived to meet the First Secretary in the early afternoon and were shown into the waiting room. After waiting for over half an hour Bernard asked me to check with security in the front hall. I was told that the person we had come to see was not yet available but they did not think we would have to wait very much longer. By the time I asked again we had been joined by another two people who were waiting to see different personnel and had been told that the people they wanted to see were tied up in a meeting. Bernard was becoming very nervous. More visitors arrived but nobody left the waiting room. Bernard thought we should not wait any longer; we were losing face. We went to the front door and said that we would have to leave, only to be told that there were good reasons for the delay and we were not going to be allowed to leave. We were escorted back to the waiting room where everyone was told to remain where they were. When the security officers left we began talking to each other about the possible reasons for our detention; most of us were very frightened. A little later a senior official came in and apologised for the ambassador. He explained that he would very shortly be telling us the reasons for the delay at a celebration he wanted to share with us and his staff. This calmed us down a little and we killed time by trying to guess the what it could be that might warrant a party.

Eventually, we were taken into the main reception room where the staff were already assembled. The ambassador announced that a Russian astronaut called Gargarin had travelled in Sputnik Vostock 1 to become the first man in space. There was great excitement in the room and some of our fellow detainees embraced each other in what I had come to know was a 'bear hug'.

The ambassador explained that they had originally expected to be able to make the announcement early in the afternoon but it had later been decided to await the results of Gargarin's medical examination before releasing the news. We all drank a toast, and were allowed to leave. It was even more exciting to hear it on the news from the car radio on my way home. I shouted to the radio: "I know!"

CHAPTER 11

A fourth class miracle

Another medical problem resulting from my fall off the scaffolding did not become apparent until sometime after the accident. An abscess appeared on the base of my spine and had to be removed. It healed well but flared up again at fairly regular intervals for some ten years or so. Although the recurrences were not accompanied by the same intensity of pain as I had experienced initially they had to be attended to. At the time of this story I was scheduled to have a further operation in about two months at the Whittington Hospital.

During that two month period my mother was diagnosed with her second cancer. The first had been in the breast and had been operated on successfully. This one was in the bladder, and she was listed for an operation by the same team due to operate on me on the same Monday morning, in the same hospital.

On the Sunday before the operation mother and I went to evening mass at our church of St Joseph's, then continued walking down Highgate Hill to the Whittington Hospital.

On the Monday morning I was the first on the list for the operating theatre. The anaesthetist decided to use a new anaesthetic which paralysed the muscles around the target area. It was based on the sap of the curare plant. Curare is still used on the tips of arrows by the natives of South America for hunting. It causes the heart and lungs of the victim to cease working. One patient in a thousand is allergic and, if this is the case, the effect of the drug is exaggerated. Parts of the body, particularly the heart, become over relaxed and the anaesthetist has difficulty in bringing the patient back after the operation. He has to wait until the drug has worked itself out of the system – that is, if you are lucky. It depends on how allergic, and how fit, you are. It would be more dangerous with someone who was old or in poor general health. In my case an operation that was scheduled for half an hour took some four hours. It was midday before I came to and the other operations were consequently delayed.

The lady anaesthetist had decided to give another patient called Murphy (my mother) on that morning's list the same drug but, after her experience with me, thinking there might be a family connection, she decided to change to another form of anaesthetic and arranged to have my mother tested for the allergy. (The anaesthetist was Indian and unaware that the hospital was in an area where a large number of Irish people lived, and that Murphy is an Irish name.)

This allergy is genetic and it was no surprise to find that the test proved positive. Mother, at that time, was in her sixties, and would have been at a much greater risk than I: it could have proved fatal. She had been saved by a most amazing set of circumstances.

I am not sure that I believe in miracles but I am sure that incidents like this do help you to see life differently. They increase your respect and appreciation for the life you have been given.

CHAPTER 12

The Catenians

Finchley Catholic Grammar School gave me a great love of the New Testament and an extensive knowledge of my faith. The residential side of school, however, failed to replace home in my spiritual and emotional development. Adherence to the religious aspects of life was based more on fear than love. The most positive effect was the rather material satisfaction I obtained from being an efficient sacristan and altar server.

When I went to college I became absorbed in architecture and the student way of life. There was a Christian Movement group I thought about joining but did not. Otherwise, there was little to remind me of religion. Very soon I stopped going to confession and communion and only went to mass to please my mother. There were, however, aspects of my faith that remained strong. I still believed in God, and I did pray – not regularly, but for specific things, mostly related to other people. I respected my conscience, even if I did not always follow it. I still took an interest in the moral issues of the day and was pleased when I found that my views coincided with those of the Church. I remember going to mass on my own, one Sunday, during a holiday in Spain, and coming away feeling very comfortable about having gone.

In my early thirties I went to Allington Castle Retreat Centre for a weekend seminar on Religious Art and Architecture. While there I was asked by the prior to design an extension to the Gilbert Scott restoration of the castle. This brought me into close contact with the Carmelite Community. Before the extension was complete I had been to confession and was attending Sunday Mass. I persevered, and a little later I felt the need to mix with other Catholics. I particularly needed to be able to discuss my faith. I remembered having once been invited by Reg Conrad to attend a Catenian dinner at The Rubens Hotel, of which he was manager – the Catenians used it for their dinner meetings. I had accepted his invitation and in the course of the evening learned that the Catenians were the result of the vision of a Manchester bishop called Casartelli, just over a hundred years ago. He had been approached for advice by workers attempting to move into management in the textile industry but who were finding it difficult to compete against those controlling the industry. They were sure that Freemasonry was a major stumbling block. He directed them to form a Catholic networking organisation. It is no coincidence that there are similarities between the two institutions.

I had been very impressed with the concept of the Catenians but did nothing about seeking to join them until the summer of 1963 when I spoke to one of the priests after mass one Sunday and he put me in touch with Hubert Cosgrove, a nice elderly widower who had been a senior civil servant for the Inland Revenue. Hubert told me he was a member of The City of London Circle but felt that I would feel more at home in a circle of younger men more related to the area in which I lived. He would introduce me to a few of the local circles. As it happened, the first circle to have its monthly meeting was his own and he took me to experience the Catenian ethos. During the evening I learnt that this circle had been created in part to assist the Archbishop of Westminster to entertain his non-clerical guests, and that the membership was made up almost entirely of members of the legal and medical professions practising in the City of London. Eight of their members had died in the past twelve months and they were keen to introduce new members below the age of fifty, which they had used as a guide in the past. They had been installing successful men; now they were prepared to introduce men they thought would become successful. And, yes, they were prepared to consider an architect with an office in the City. I told them that evening that I would like to join. They made me very welcome. I was, however, conscious that their friendly conversation was designed to find out more about me. One of their customs was to ask prospective members to entertain them with several after dinner speeches during the twelve months before a formal interview with the nominating committee. It is no wonder that the circle had a reputation for producing after dinner speakers. If you did not like making such speeches you would certainly not have wanted to join this circle.

The membership is now more broadly representative of those who work in the City and we have many accountants and people involved in finance and insurance. The unifying factor is that we do all work, or did work, or have close connections with the City of London. Our meetings were originally held in Sion College Library on the Embankment, and later at The Law Society. Unfortunately, costs drove us out of the City to Simpsons in the Strand, and now we are at the Lansdowne Club, just off Berkeley Square.

Very few of us actually live in the City. We travel in from as far as fifty miles away. It is, therefore, a circle that limits all but one of its activities to a weekday evening in the Lansdowne Club. Our monthly meetings are held in a three room suite, consisting of a meeting room, bar, and dining room. Three of the meetings commence in the suite but adjourn for dinner in the ballroom. Here we entertain the parish priests of the City in February, the wives and families in July, and Her Majesty's Catholic Judges in October. Numerically this is our biggest and grandest event. We recently entertained twenty-five Judges and some eighty other Catenian guests, most of them from the legal profession.

In recent times members have chosen to involve us in their personal charities. Bill Metcalf puts on a charity ball in the summer, and Mike Bedford takes some of our members to Lourdes each year. But, apart from these contributions, we do not as Catenians do anything for the Church or the community.

Although we do not live near each other there are other things that bind us. A significant number of our members are related one to another. Some are a third generation of membership, and among my closest companions in the circle are the sons of old friends now no longer with us. We also meet through other Catholic organisations where we are making a more active contribution to the life of the church. It certainly achieves what I was looking for: somewhere I can discuss the Catholic issues of the day.

I was the president in 1985 and the highlight of my year was the dinner to honour Cardinal Archbishop Basil Hume OSB who had taught some of our members, and Sir Alan Davis, a member who was Lord Mayor of London that year. Sir Alan was happy to take second place to Cardinal Hume, particularly as we were now meeting outside the City. We did, however, have two receptions. I introduced the members to the Cardinal, and my deputy introduced them to Sir Alan. They sat on either side of me at dinner and each gave a short address. It was a truly memorable evening.

One of the aims of the association is for its members to get to know a much wider range of the membership than are contained in one member's own circle. This is achieved by visiting other circles. In mine, however, we have (alas!) a reputation for not visiting other circles, but we compensate by being a popular one for Catenians from other circles. I have also got to know a large number of Catenians by attending some of our national events. I have been to three AGMs and was an after dinner speaker at banquets in Brighton and Newcastle. In the latter city I had the dubious honour of sitting on the top table with members of the City Council involved in the John Poulson and T. Dan Smith corruption affair.

Two other very memorable Catenian occasions were the circle meetings to celebrate the 100th anniversary of the first meeting of the first circle in Manchester on the 16th May, 1908. There were over 500 of us present, with all the living past presidents seated on either side of the Grand President. The second was the 100th anniversary dinner of the first meeting of the first circle to be formed in London on the 19th December, 1909. Over 200 sat down to dinner. An extra incentive for my attendance at these two events was something that the presiding presidents had in common: the Grand President, David Taylor, at the first celebration, was once a member of the London Serra, and Peter Wurr, the club president at the second event, is the present president of the London Serra, another Catholic organisation of which I am a member and which I shall discuss later.

There is great pleasure to be gained from meeting a group of like-minded people at regular intervals over a long period of time. You develop a relationship which is close to that experienced in a good family gathering. The knowledge you share brings you very close, and the longer you continue to share it the closer you get.

CHAPTER 13

Serra

Hubert Cosgrove, who had introduced me to the Catenians, also introduced me to Frank Lloyd, a principal in Brunsdens Ltd, a Highgate firm of building contractors. Frank was a Catenian in another circle; he served daily mass in our church, and became a kind of surrogate father to me. He enjoyed giving me advice on how to get on in life and introducing me to people who might help me to do so. This relationship could have been very important if it had helped to expand my practice but it was not that appropriate. The only time we actually worked together was to design and build a chapel at the nursing home in Hornsey Lane, the first time I used polished rough green Cornish slate. It was this same slate that became the focus of the brand image for Allied Irish Bank in England.

It was Frank who introduced me to Serra, a group of lay Catholics devoted to fostering and supporting vocations to the priesthood and religious life. Serra had begun life in Seattle USA in 1935, a time when Catholic organisations were named after their patrons. There was no American saint, so they chose America's most famous priest, blessed Friar Junipero Serra. He had been chaplain to the Spanish army that colonised the west coast of America in the late 1770s, his particular role being to stabilise the areas conquered by the army as they proceeded up the California coast. He achieved this by constructing mission stations three days' walk apart, an arrangement designed to help the army, with the help of the Franciscans, to control the American Indians. These missions were walled areas of farmland with craft workshops and accommodation built around a church and monastery. They allowed Junipero Serra and his Franciscan Friars to train the Indians to be good craftsmen and farmers whilst they endeavoured to convert them to Christianity. The missions were successful and by the end of the century had become villages.

These villages expanded and grew into the towns of California, towns which, although most of the farm buildings and some of the churches have been lost or replaced, still bear their original names. Starting from the Mexican border they are: San Diego, San Luis Rey, San Juan Capistrano, San Buenaventura (Ventura), San Gabriel, Los Angeles, Archangel, Santa Barbara, San Luis Obispo, San Miguel, San Carlos Borromeo (Carmel), Santa Cruz, Santa Clara, San Rafael Archangel, San José and San Francisco. I have visited all of them at least once, and on three occasions I have visited Fra Junipero's birth place in Petra Majorca. He has become a very important companion.

Frank Lloyd was the acting president of our prospective group, trying to recruit the twenty-five members necessary to start a Serra club in London. I was a response to that recruitment drive. We were formally chartered on Guy Fawkes' night in 1966 at the Irish Club in Eton Place. It was a memorable and inspiring evening.

Serra became the rock that supported my faith and provided the context for some of the most exciting events of my life. Our activites consisted of organising vocation masses, vigils, retreats, exhibitions, surveys, altar servers' awards, Sixth

Form talks, programmes for teachers, seminars for heads of Religious Education and heads of schools. Probably the most important of our programmes was The 31 Club. We were given permission by our diocese to speak from the ambo at the point in the mass where a homily would normally be preached. We would talk for five minutes on the importance of 'vocation' in our lives, the important part parents play in fostering Christian vocation in their children's lives, and the particular part the whole laity have in fostering the special vocation of priesthood and the religious life. A further two minutes was allowed to introduce The 31 Club. The congregation were asked to commit themselves as individuals or as a family to attend mass once a month to pray that someone in the parish would hear a call to priesthood or the religious life. Those who agreed would provide their contact details at the back of the church after mass and a poster showing their names against the allocated days of the month would be produced and put up at the back of the church before the following Sunday. Our expectation was to sign up about fourteen per cent of the mass attendance.

Some of our work we did with the Vocation Sisters and I became an adviser to their first Superior. When they decided to work with priests, brothers and nuns who had difficulty in living in their communities after Vatican II, I was asked to become Chairman of Governors of the Angmering House. The professional and religious involved in the healing process were all entering into a new field, and together they worked towards producing some very successful results. The governors were expected to attend some of the evaluation days and it was very satisfying to be part of the system.

A member of the committee was the Passionist priest, William Kenny, now Auxiliary Bishop for the Archdiocese of Birmingham. In those days he travelled from his diocese in Scandinavia to our bi-annual meetings. He would stay at St Joseph's in Highgate and I would pick him up there on my way to Angmering. On one of these occasions I was turning into Park Lane from Oxford Street very early one Saturday morning when I was overtaken by a police car, siren screaming. I stopped; the police car stopped. The officer told me to get out of my car and join him on the pavement. He accused me of speeding, asked for my licence, and proceeded to create the paperwork. I had nothing to say in my defence, so he handed me my copy and I continued down Park Lane. As I reached the Hilton I heard the siren again. He pulled up in front of me and I stopped. Again he asked me to get out of the car and join him on the pavement. I did so. "As you drove off I caught sight of your passenger's ring," he said. "Is he a bishop?" I told him he was. "I wouldn't have been responsible for my actions in your position," he replied, tore up the paperwork and walked off.

Another role associated with my being in Serra started with a phone call from Monsignor John Coghlan, Rector of the diocesan seminary. He had just returned from a meeting of seminary rectors, at which they had questioned the validity of the present system for accepting candidates for the priesthood. They were unhappy with its being limited to an interview with the bishop of the diocese assisted by the Vocation Director and the Seminary Rector. They thought that the secular use of residential selection conferences for the choice of candidates was worth considering. He wanted me to set up a think tank of Serrans to see how this concept could be put into practice. I agreed and eventually, with two other Serrans and Monsignor John, I sat down to a good dinner at the 'San Carlo' in Highgate to discuss the matter. Monsignor John explained that the Cardinal would still be making the decision, but it was felt that the advice he was presently receiving should be supplemented by a detailed assessment of the candidate made by representatives of the Church.

The first decisions we arrived at proposed the greatest difference to the existing system. The selection weekend would involve three interviewers: a layman, a laywoman, and a priest. The interviews would be on a one-to-one basis, and should take about an hour. It was thought that the Catholic Marriage Advisory Service might be a useful source of potential interviewers, and it was agreed there should be some form of training. After three of these dinners, we had the basis for a proposal to put to the Cardinal. All that was left were the details of designing the application forms and marking systems. A particular management consultant in the Catenians was felt to be the best man to comment on our approach and advise on the detailed arrangements for the weekend of interviews.

Shortly after the meetings with Monsignor John, Fr Kevin Kenny, the head of the Communications Department at Ushaw College, asked me if I would be prepared to be an interviewer at a new form of selection of candidates for the eight northern dioceses at Ushaw. I said I would and went up to see Monsignor Peter Cookson, the Rector of the seminary. It was the first time I had been in this very impressive neo-gothic building where they still employed elderly gentlemen, called 'coal boys', who took coal donated by the mines to the fires in the rooms. It was built for a large number of students and rooms were commodious and high-ceilinged. It was not exactly cosy, but it was a college you could enjoy studying in. The grounds were large and far enough away from the nearest village to provide the necessary separation from the distractions of modern life.

Their selection conference was based on a similar concept to the one we had designed for Westminster, but we were given no training. We were told only what they were trying to achieve. It certainly differed from the type of job interview with which I was familiar. The college was looking for men who could live simply and cope with a wide cross section of society. They would have to work for long hours in a long week without either direction or the support of a family home. The applicants would have to understand, and be comfortable with, celibacy. It was left to the interviewers to find the questions that would bring out the answers. Many of these were intensely personal and the task would have proved acutely embarrassing were it not for the attitude of the candidates. The younger ones were able to take the questions in their stride, while the older ones tended to be more diffident. What we learnt from the interviews was augmented by time spent with the candidates at meals and in the evening.

We never worked with fewer than two teams of interviewers, and each team would interview about nine candidates on the Saturday. On Sunday morning the interviewers met with the Seminary Rector and the Vocation Director. In order to ensure that assessments were not influenced by the opinions of the other members of the team, each interviewer would state his mark before any assessment was given. When all assessments had been presented the interviewers and the Rector would enter the debate to produce a one page final assessment. The final marks awarded by the interviewers could be changed if any wished to revise their thinking after the debate.

In the early days of this new system the bishops accepted some of candidates we had not recommended. This was understandable because of the shortage of vocations, but after some of these had left the seminary of their own accord (or had been asked to leave), the bishops became more appreciative of our findings.

When Fr Kevin left the Seminary to become parish priest of Pleasington I resigned. I had been driving up to Ushaw three times a year for some eight or nine years. Most of the selection conferences were in the winter and I was finding the drive at the end of a strenuous weekend very difficult.

I had only been out of the process at Ushaw for a few months, however, when the Westminster Vocations Director, Fr Michael Johnston, asked me to be an interviewer for my own diocese. This was a little different, because the weekend involved interviewing for only one diocese, the programme was designed by the Vocation Director, and we had a more direct relationship with our archbishop. There are now many priests I meet in my own diocese whom I have interviewed. A few of them give me the impression that they feel a bit uncomfortable in my presence, but this is compensated for by my relationship with the majority, which I think is rather special.

In certain circumstances special interviews were held outside the regular programme, and a laywoman and I were asked on one occasion to interview two candidates retiring from work closely associated with the diocese, and on another occasion the first two Neo-Catechumenate candidates for priesthood in the diocese.

We used to have meetings and seminars to give consideration to particular aspects of our work, and we once invited Jack Dominion to talk to us about the subject of homosexuality and the priesthood. He was very sure of his thinking and we had no difficulty in accepting it. He was convinced that the selection process should treat homosexuals in the same way as heterosexuals. The key issue was not sexuality but celibacy. We had to satisfy ourselves that all candidates were able to be celibate. Past experience indicated that problems arose only in seminaries with a disproportionate number of homosexuals.

Very shortly after I joined Serra I was appointed by the

National Council of Serra to be their representative on JOVAC, the Joint Vocation Council, which included Vocation Directors from the dioceses and from the male and female religious orders. We met at the Jesuit House in Farm Street. Then came a separation of the diocesan directors from the religious, and I became a member of the Religious Directors of Vocation, while Jack Andrews was our representative on the National Conference of Secular Vocation Directors. After some five or six years I took over his role, and attended all their conferences until 2005 when I ceased to be their representative.

The National Conference of Vocation Directors' sub-committees meet fairly frequently, but the full conference meets only once a year for a week in one of the three English or two Roman seminaries, or at the Spanish seminary, though we have also made occasional visits to other seminaries of interest. Among these were the non-diocesan seminary with a waiting list in Ars, France; the Irish seminary at Maynooth, Eire, that had since 1795 ordained some 10,000 priests for most parts of the world; the seminary outside Rome where our students used to spend their summers; and the Carthusian monastery at Parkminster, where the monks studying for the priesthood do so in their own cells, with a weekly visit from a fellow monk for half an hour.

We did not stay at Parkminster. We spent a day there during our conference in the seminary at Wonersh. I had heard that the Carthusian monk lived a silent life on his own in a cell, and I had visualised the monastery consisting of very basic cells separated from each other and the church they served. That was not what we found. The prior who welcomed us had a fairly elaborate series of rooms, which enabled him to offer hospitality to monastery guests. The monastery was very large and the cloisters giving access to the 'cells' were so long that monks used bikes to get around. I was surprised to find that there were lay brothers who lived silently in community, providing the services that supported the monastery. They lived together as monks and brothers do in other religious houses. The cloister monks occupied their own cells within a very solid stone building on two floors, with access from the cloister. The entrance gave access to a corridor running parallel to the cloister and alongside an enclosed garden for the individual monk's cultivation and exercise. At the end of the corridor and garden was a workshop at ground level, and a staircase to the upper level. Here there were two adjoining rooms. The first was furnished with a table and chair for eating. The second had a built in bed and prie-dieu in beautifully carved timber. There was also a toilet with a shower, thanks to English Heritage, but it was not something we were shown. The monk's food was placed in a small cupboard built into the wall of the cloister. It was because the cell and garden took up so much space that the cloisters were so long. The monk left the cell daily for mass and night office, and on Saturdays for the community four hour walk in the countryside, the one time in the week when the cloistered monk can communicate with his fellow religious. It was a fascinating day, and gave much food for thought.

An issue which caused alarm in the church at the beginning of 2010 first surfaced in our country in 1998 at the annual meeting of the National Conference of Vocation Directors. One of the speakers at the conference was a psychiatrist and one of problems he spoke about was paedophilia. He explained that although the practice had always existed it had only just been accepted that it was not something that could be treated. Any priest suffering from such tendencies should be removed from his priestly role immediately. He made a special point of telling the vocation directors present that they should be extremely careful in the selection of candidates and made some suggestions as to what they should look for. During the question time that followed it became clear that no one in the room had heard the word 'paedophile' before or realised that this form of abuse was untreatable.

When the National Conference prepared its report for presentation to the next bishops' conference, particular emphasis was placed on paedophilia and a strong recommendation made that the subject be discussed with a view to providing guidelines. I know this was acted upon shortly afterwards, and the Nolan Committee set up in 2000.

Now that we were aware of the problem the interviewing panels studied the characteristics of candidates and began to ask appropriate questions. I am sure that our awareness of the problems of the past, and the concept of the selection conference will act as a safeguard for the future.

Much of our thinking in Serra raises questions without clear answers. Why are men and women still prepared to devote their lives to a celibate life of unselfish work? We know from surveys that about fourteen per cent of young Catholic boys think about priesthood at some time in their lives. What can we Serrans say and do to encourage them to come forward? Why do we find it so difficult to get men and women to join us in our efforts in Serra? They agree that it is an important apostolic work, and that there is now a noticeable shortage of priests, but the English Catholic does not want to get involved in it. There is something about the gulf we have created in this country between the clergy and the laity which leads people to think that all priestly things should be left to priests. Even many priests believe this. There is also a new post-Vatican II gulf between the committed Catholic who goes to mass every Sunday and whose conscience leads him to seek a deeper participation in the Christian life, and others who attend mass regularly but do not think they are good enough to get involved and that everything except hearing the masses should be left to the pious ones.

Most of the work I have done for the Church has been at diocesan level. Even when, as Serrans, we are working in the parishes, we are responsible to the bishops and the diocese. Consequently, I have always felt that I was missing something by not being an active member of the parish, so a few years ago I decided to do something about it. The next time the parish form for offers of help came round I took it seriously. Extra help was being asked for everything: eucharistic ministers, readers, altar servers, members of the choir, money collectors, money counters, receptionists, church cleaners. I really did not mind what I did, so I ticked all the boxes and left it to them. What I had not realised was that there was someone in charge of each area and my name had been given to each one of them. They were soon on the phone and I had to make a choice. I ended up choosing one each from the top, the middle, and the bottom of the list. I became a minister of the eucharist who collected the money at mass and cleaned the church once a month. I had to give up the cleaning a few years ago because of my health, but I am still a minister and a collector and have added 'member of the finance committee' to my list of responsibilities. I have certainly got to know many more people, and I do now feel very much part of the parish community.

CHAPTER 14

The Submariner

I was down in Devon with Clem Shepherd visiting Sue and her husband Bill. They had both been keen on horses and all equestrian sports and it was probably that which brought them together. However, Bill had lost a hand in some farm machinery, which stopped him riding. It did not stop him farming and looking after the horses, however. Sue was riding in a point to point that weekend and we picnicked from the back of their shooting-brake. While we were having lunch a rather jolly chap came to say 'hello' to Sue and wish her luck in her race. We were introduced. He was the captain of the first nuclear submarine. During the conversation that followed Gibraltar was mentioned, and Spain, and Clem and I realised we would be there at the same time as the captain, he prior to a good will tour of the Spanish Mediterranean coast in the nuclear submarine he captained, and we in a hired car we intended to pick up to tour around southern Spain. (All this was to take place after the announcement that England and Spain had resolved their difficulties over ownership of Gibraltar. As it happened, however, the convention never did manage to resolve those difficulties and the British fleet spent most of the summer in Gibraltar.) We agreed to meet in Gibraltar.

When we flew onto The Rock we picked up a Seat, a Spanish

version of the Fiat, and drove down to the naval dockyard, arriving in early afternoon. The police station is just inside the gate and we were stopped by a policeman in an older version of the uniform our own police wore at the time. He told us in no uncertain terms that the Spanish car could not enter the English dockyard. Did we not realise that Gibraltar was not on speaking terms with Spain or the Spanish? We must leave it outside in the street, then come back to the police station. When we returned, the officials were quite polite and said they would tell the captain we had arrived. When he appeared we told him the story, and he tried to get our car into the dockyard but they were adamant and even he had to admit defeat.

We walked down to the submarine and could see that there was a party in full swing on the deck. This was amazing because the vessel itself was cylindrical and the flat part of the deck limited in width to no more than about five feet. It was full of people and there were no handrails. When we got nearer we could see that the only way onto the deck was via a collapsible gangplank no more than a foot wide with a swinging wire handrail on one side only. It was not so frightening once one had had a few drinks, but it was sufficiently dangerous to make everyone careful. When the party was over and people had left, we were taken below for a tour.

It is amazing to see just how little space people can live in. The captain, who is the only member of the crew to have any privacy, lives in a space 5.5 x 4.5 feet, consisting of a bunk in front of which is a 2 x 2 foot space. The remainder of the bunk length is taken up with a cupboard which opens on all sides. The 2 x 2 foot space is where the captain stands, sits and changes his clothes. He works sitting on the bunk with his legs in this space. A working-top folds down to cover his lap. The cupboard has to hold his summer and winter uniforms as well as the ship's bookwork. The other officers share a room with a table in the centre; the walls are lined with their bunks, stacked one above the other. Here they have to eat and work, not infrequently spending as long as six months at sea.

We were taken through the ship to see the kitchens, and the various work stations where the men sleep in their hammocks. The most frightening place to me was the sealed area that houses the nuclear power unit. To live that close to nuclear fission must be awesome. It was more frightening to think about than the torpedo tubes. These were transformed into an acceptable piece of furniture by being covered with a snorkel kit and a pair of swimming trunks laid out to dry!

We were also shown the fittings on the side of the hull where a member of the crew would be strapped when the submarine was on the move. He had broken his leg in a football match they had played against another ship, but he had chosen to stay with the submarine rather than take sick leave.

That evening we said 'goodbye' to the captain and drove to our luxurious Hotel Queen Victoria in La Línea de la Concepción on the Spanish mainland. The next day we were eating the most fabulous lobster salad lunch on the terrace of the hotel when we received a message from the captain. He had decided to come over that evening to show us the town. Accordingly, although we had intended to leave that day we cancelled our next hotel and booked in for an additional night. It was well worth it. We had an excellent meal and ended up in a night club where he was obviously well known and where he showed off his dance skills with a flamenco. Early next morning he left us and I have never seen him since.

CHAPTER 15

Canon Kevin

The most important spiritual influence in my life has come from my friendship with The Very Revd Canon Kevin Kenny, parish priest of Pleasington Priory, Trustee and Canon of the Diocese of Salford, Honorary Canon of the Holy Sepulchre in Jerusalem and Ecumenical Canon of the Anglican Cathedral in Blackburn. He was just Fr Kevin when I first knew him in the early '70s but already holding the important positions of Bishop's Secretary and Director of Vocations for the diocese. I met him at the national meetings of Vocation Directors and at Serra gatherings. He attended most of our Serra national meetings and was very supportive. He was also the keynote speaker at two of the International Serra conventions in the USA, where he was a great success. I particularly enjoyed the comment of one American lady, delivered in a very strong trans-Atlantic accent: "I like the way you talk our language."

After he became a Knight of the Holy Sepulchre he would stay at my flat for the national investitures. He would also occasionally spend a night at the flat on his way through London when staying with the Kinches or Monsignor Peter Strand, both good friends and fellow Knights.

On one occasion I was driving to France with Monsignor Peter to meet Fr Kevin for a short holiday. We were held up at Dover, waiting for the weather to improve – but it did not improve and we were forced to spend the night in a hotel. By the time we drove onto the ferry the next day I had spent some nine hours in the car with the Monsignor. It is amazing how much you get to know about each other in those circumstances. He chose to tell me about his priesthood – the good parts and the difficult ones. This was a very moving experience for somebody who had only recently found his way back to the Church.

When Fr Kevin ceased to be Bishop's Secretary he was appointed to teach communication at Ushaw College and I was with him three times a year for the selection conferences. I was also able to take on a commission to reorder the Sanctuary at Our Lady Immaculate and St Cuthbert in Crook, for which Fr Kevin had recommended me. The church had been designed by John Francis Bentley, the architect of Westminster Cathedral. It was the first time I had attempted a reordering, and the first time I had worked on a listed building.

On another occasion Father Kevin was entertaining the International President of Serra, Frank Metyko, and his wife Rita at Ushaw one weekend. They lived in Houston and had never before stayed in such an old building. There was much to fascinate them in the seminary but the memory they most frequently referred to was of their first morning when they came down to breakfast to see us making our toast with toasting forks over the open fire in the refectory.

It was easy for Fr Kevin to fill the summer vacations but for Christmas he would stay with me in the flat. This enabled us to have the three masses of Christmas. We invited friends and neighbours to the midnight mass and the third mass at noon. We then had our traditional Christmas party. The custom of holding this before our Christmas lunch was an old one started by my brother and me when we were teenagers. In later years mother, Fr Kevin and I were joined for the party and lunch by Fr Frank Hegarty, the chaplain of the London Serra.

At one of these parties I bought Fr Kevin a 'crock pot' and showed him how to use it, so that for the times when he knew he was going to miss a meal at the seminary he would not have to take something cold from the refrigerator. This gift created his first interest in cooking and he soon became quite adventurous.

When he left the seminary, Fr Kevin became parish priest of Pleasington and Feniscowles, situated between Blackburn and Preston. He loves these villages and he loves being parish priest. He has got to know everyone who lives there and has no problem in remembering their names and everything about them – a great gift which enables him to be a father to the area in a very real sense.

The church at Feniscowles was relatively new but that at Pleasington, although a very attractive gothic building, had several design problems and was in poor condition. I was asked to resolve the problems and reorder the sanctuary. The plaster was poor and covered in damp stains, so I removed it, exposing very good stonework. Now, although the stonework still gets damp it no longer shows. The plaster has not been replaced!

The church had no form of lobby, the front door opening directly into the nave. This made the building very cold. Accordingly, I enclosed an area at the back of the church with glass in slim, anodised aluminium framing. Thus protected from the wind, the church is now warm. The apse at the end of the nave had beautiful stained glass windows above the altar, but very ugly relief sculpture below them, so we covered the sculpture with linen panels in the liturgical colours, and these now make an attractive backing for the new matching stone altar, ambo and chair. This last item of furniture was placed in front of the column on one side of the apse, where it has assumed an even greater significance in this church because Fr Kevin always gives his sermon seated in it. (He is also known for illustrating his sermons with references to scenes from the latest episodes of TV soaps.)

The wooden floor of the sanctuary was suffering from dry rot so we planned to replace it. This led to some of the older parishioners telling Fr Kevin the story of the relic. Instead of a small piece of a saint being put within the altar, the Lord of the Manor, Francis Butler had gone to Rome and purchased a whole saint who had been buried under the wooden floor below the altar. Nobody really believed this story, but when the builders took up the sanctuary floor they found a strange package wrapped in oilcloth. Before we had opened the package Fr Kevin told the parish at mass on Sunday that the relics of the saint might have been found. Someone in the congregation gave the story to the local press and the police chose to interpret the situation differently. A special opening of the package in the presence of the police and coroner had to be arranged. When the wrappings were removed and the remains exposed and tested, it was decided that the information on the label found between the layers was almost certainly correct. It declared the remains to be those of a young Christian martyr, probably killed in the Coliseum. The relics were reverently enclosed in a timber coffin within the new altar and this can be glimpsed though openings in the Jerusalem cross relief sculpture on the front of the altar, a design chosen because of Fr Kevin's connection with the Patriarchate of Jerusalem and the Order of the Holy Sepulchre.

Some time after the work was finished Fr Kevin asked me to produce a drawing for an architectural foldaway stable for his Christmas crib, to be made by one of the parishioners. I think it must have been my smallest commission.

During his very active life Fr Kevin has been chaplain to the National Council of the laity, spiritual director on numerous pilgrimages to the Holy Land for the Equestrian Order of the Holy Sepulchre, as well as director of many retreats for the clergy and others. He has also acted as guide and mentor to a large number of seminarians studying for the priesthood in the Patriarchate of Jerusalem. These activities have brought many of those with whom he has come into contact to his parish in Pleasington, where his parishioners are always ready to extend their hospitality to such guests, and gain much from their acquaintance. One of the ways some of us were able to repay this hospitality was to partake in a series of Lenten talks on our journey of faith, and if the other speakers put as much of themselves into theirs as I did into mine the parish was well rewarded. It was something I was doing for the first time, and I gained enormously from the exercise.

I have frequently thought about a vocation to the priesthood but when, on one occasion, I talked to Fr Kevin about it his answer was quick and short: "You are already spending most of your time involved in the church. It would be crazy to spend five years doing nothing but studying for what you might be less capable of doing." As far as he was concerned that was the end of the discussion. He has, however, always been very supportive of what I do, and I was particularly pleased that he agreed to be the principal celebrant at the nuptial mass when I got married.

CHAPTER 16

Highgate

Highgate Village is perched on a hill overlooking the City of London, just five miles away. Fabulous views of the city can be had from many of our open spaces. In days gone by, people coming to London from the North would have travelled by horse drawn carriage, and the last stop for many of them would have been Highgate Village. Here, the locals made them welcome by providing a washing pond for the coaches to drive through, shops to buy clothes or wigs in, and places to get things cleaned or otherwise attended to. For those staying overnight there were nineteen inns to choose from. If on the following morning they still had enough money to pay the toll, they could pass through the gate at the bottom of the hill and continue their journey into the big city.

It was only a stone's throw from the bottom of Highgate Hill to the flat my parents lived in when I was born. The toll gate had gone and public transport to the City took the form of trams, like those found in San Francisco. Our present basement car park is where the engine that powered the cable was housed.

When my father died the rest of the family moved back to Highgate. We purchased the bottom half of a substantial four storey house in Stanhope Road, part of the last extension to the east of the old village of Highgate made at the beginning of the twentieth century. I am still here and I do not want to leave. One of the most successful developments my company undertook was a block of twenty flats in this area at the corner of Stanhope Road and Shepherds Hill. I have also completed eight other commissions in Highgate, probably more than any other architect.

Highgate village still retains the character of a village. It has many shops in premises built in past centuries. Twelve of the original inns still exist. The washing pond has been filled in to satisfy those locals who were fearful of infections from the stagnant water. It was sad to lose it, and many of us tried to have it restored, but its absence has proved to be an even more important asset, for the space it occupied has become the village square and the centre of village activity. One of our buses starts and stops there. Our festivals and other displays are held in the square, or in the adjoining buildings. It is where the donkey carrying Mary to the inn begins his journey, and where we sing our Christmas carols under the Christmas lights. In the spring Harringtons sell plants once a week there and in June we have a fair.

Two important buildings in the square house the Highgate Society and the Highgate Scientific and Literary institute. The Highgate Society performs the same function as a village council, and the meeting place becomes the village hall. The Highgate Scientific and Literary Institute was created in 1839 and preceded the Public Library. It houses, among other items of interest, some of the work of Highgate's past and present inhabitants. I was a member of both organisations and on the environmental committee of the Society for a while. Now I am simply a member of the Society. My wife is more active in both the Society and the Institute.

We have four churches, a hospital, a tea shop, two coffee

bars, six restaurants, two banks, and all the shops we need. The only regrets we have are the loss of our post office and the growth of estate agents in the High Street. They speak for the popularity of the place.

This was the last home my brother Derek knew. It was in our lounge that we celebrated his last return to duty.

I was eventually able to purchase the top half of the house, move the office down to Holloway and then convert the whole house into four two-bedroom, self-contained flats. I had the ground floor, mother had the garden flat, and I sold the other two to pay for the conversion. It was the first time I had lived in a flat on my own and I thoroughly enjoyed it. We could each still do for the other those things we did best. In retrospect I realise that I had the better deal. Mother did the gardening, the shopping, and the laundry; I just helped with a few odd jobs, and did the cooking on Sundays and when guests were invited. Mother and I got on better being this much apart.

When my practice designed the new offices in Highgate Village the Greater London Planning authority insisted on our providing two flats over the offices, in order to ensure that the expansion of office building in London did not eliminate a residential presence. One day, during the building of our offices, I was standing on what was to be the floor of the flats, admiring the view which was magnificent from that height. So good was it that I decided there and then to purchase the flats from my partner. I made one of them as large as possible and connected it to the correspondingly smaller one which, with its own shower room and kitchenette, is suitable for guests. Because it opens off the office staircase it can also be used as my office.

The larger flat does not share an entrance with the offices, but has its own entrance with a ground floor hall. This gives access to a private lift which carries you up four floors to a spacious living area enclosed on the south and west with full-height sliding windows. These provide the most magnificent views of London: the Olympic village to the east, Canary Wharf, the City, and Westminster to the west. The windows also give access to planted terraces which look down over Waterlow Park and the Village. The bedrooms face east and catch the early morning sun. They have a planted terrace and wonderful views of Alexandra Palace. Our lift also goes to the basement where we have a wine cellar and can use the basement car park.

The location is excellent. We are only two minutes' walk from the bus stop, ten minutes from the tube, five minutes from St Joseph's, our parish church, and within three minutes of all the shops we need.

When I moved into the flats over the offices mother took my flat in Stanhope road, which enabled me to sell the garden flat to help with my new mortgage. Unfortunately, this turned out to be a mistake because my flat had many steps – steps up to the entrance, steps between the split level living area and kitchen, and steps down to the garden where mother spent most of her time. As she reached ninety I thought all these steps presented too great a risk, so I encouraged her to move into warden assisted accommodation nearby in Muswell Hill. She missed the garden, but very soon became involved in creating a small plot from the grass area adjoining her new flat.

CHAPTER 17

Illness

I have never found illness difficult, possibly because I normally plan a holiday at the end of it. The first illness I can remember was the pleurisy I took with me on my first trip to Paris. My GP had only discovered it the day before I left with some college friends who had exciting reasons for going there. I thought if I took things easy I could still go, and I did. I did not see much of the normal tourist sites, however, because I spent most of the days in bed getting over the previous night and building up enough strength to go out with the group the following night. It is, therefore, only the exciting evenings spent at the Folies Bergère and various restaurants that remain in my memory.

My first operation was in the late fifties. It was to remove a cist on my goitre. I went into Saints John & Elizabeth Hospital in St John's Wood for the operation. The nurses made a great fuss of me and I thoroughly enjoyed it. When I was fit enough to get up, Matron wanted me to recuperate in a convalescent home – one always went away for recuperation after an operation in those days. I was able to persuade her to let me go straight home, where my mother would look after me. This was not quite the truth, however, as I had actually decided to take myself by car to Brittany for a few days. I had put the car in a garage for a service, with the intention of having it brought to the hospital to pick me up; I had told Matron that I would be picked up by a hired car. This was just as well because she came to see me off at the hospital entrance. All I had to do was stop the garage man getting out of the driving seat until we had gone around the corner. I then drove to Dover. Here I had to find a passport photograph machine in order to obtain a temporary passport from the post office. By the time I had located the only machine in Dover, the post office was shut. I was just about to seek a hotel for the night when a man came out of the post office and started to bolt the door. Throwing myself on his mercy, I asked whether he could feel sorry for a poor convalescent just out of hospital and fix me up with a passport. I think he was so staggered that anyone should imagine he would go back after closing time that he agreed to open up for me. As a result, I was able to catch the ferry, and book into a good hotel in Boulogne instead of having to stay the night in Dover. The next few fabulous days were spent touring Brittany.

★ ★ ★

On the first day of January 1988 I went into the office expecting to be alone, only to find my business partner, Ron, had also chosen to come in. During a chat over coffee he asked me if I realised that my voice was occasionally very low and husky. I said that it was to be expected after the heavy drinking of the previous night, but he told me he had noticed it happening for a while and had discussed it with a medical friend whose advice was that I should see my GP. I was sufficiently concerned to do so and he sent me to Michael MacKinnon, an Ear, Nose and Throat specialist in Harley Street, who examined me and recommended an operation to remove an unidentifiable growth. This procedure took place in the clinic on his premises, and I was home after twenty-four hours. (Michael has since commissioned the practice to carry out certain improvements to his property in Harley Street and we have become good friends.)

On the day I was due to see Michael for the result of the operation I drove to Harley Street and arrived rather early. As I waited in a metered parking bay I thought about the possible result of the operation and how I would handle it. I was convinced I had cancer. The chances of recovery in those days were not as good as they are today, so I thought I should perhaps go to confession. Then I realised that if my life was going to be that short I would be able to report to God directly. Strangely, I felt then that I could cope with cancer if that was what it turned out to be.

I left the car and walked to Michael's office. I was even able to concentrate on the magazine I was reading in the waiting room. When Michael's receptionist called my name I climbed the long flight of stairs to his office. I was quite calm. I remained calm when he explained that what he had removed from my throat was a cancerous growth on the vocal cords and I would have to undergo a course of radiotherapy six days a week for six weeks at the Royal Free Hospital in Hampstead.

The consultant at the Royal Free carried out various tests to see how much radiation I could take and made the necessary arrangements for me to have the thirty-six sessions, ending on Maundy Thursday. I was able to have some say in deciding my own time of day. My first choice was first thing in the morning, but this slot was already taken, at least initially, so I had to go in the afternoon for a few days before the 9.00 am slot became free. Cancer patients are treated especially well and I was able to use one of the two parking spaces reserved for those who could drive themselves, which enabled me to get to the office by ten o'clock.

The most difficult part of the treatment was constructing the protective mask. It is made of a kind of plastic which covers the whole head. The liquid plastic is poured onto plastic sheeting fixed close to the head. The final mould has breathing holes, and an opening for the radiation. Around this opening, lines are drawn, that enable the therapist to line up the source of the radiation. The mask is also split at the back, each side of the slit being fixed to a flange. The process does not hurt; it is just very claustrophobic. It is also not helped by one's Adam's apple. I was unaware that it moved until I had the mask on. It was sufficiently tight to impair this movement and that was very frightening. The marvellous men and women who work in this area are extremely patient and they take time to explain everything, which helps you to accept the difficulties. One is placed inside the mask and helped up a step onto a platform. From here one climbs onto a wooden bed. The flanges of the mask are bolted to a wooden block on the bed. This ensures that you cannot move your head. The bed then slides into the radiation tunnel, the staff leave and the radiation is turned on. It would have taken more than my thirty-six sessions for me to get inured to it. It is very unpleasant.

At some time during the series of treatments my friend John Evans made a generous and important offer. He would take me to the Masters golf tournament in Augusta if I completed the sessions. This event takes place just after Easter – perfect timing for an incentive. It encouraged me to continue working through the course, while driving myself to the hospital, running my practice, completing my studies for the arbitration degree, and sitting as a magistrate.

It was a rule that male magistrates must always wear ties when sitting on the bench. After quite a short period of time, however, I was unable to do this. My neck had become raw and tender, so I managed to get permission to wear a loose cravat instead. This was important to me because I felt that I had to carry on as normal. A few of the solicitors and barristers approached the clerks to discover whether this depreciation of standards was acceptable, but once the situation was explained to them I ceased to be disreputable and became a hero.

The Saturday before my last week, the nurse in charge of my treatment said that the radiation was having too severe an effect on my skin, the neck had become too raw, and I must go and see my consultant who would probably decide to stop the treatment for a while. The idea of having to stop and start again did not appeal to me and I feared I might lose my chance of going to the Masters. On the Monday there was a new nurse in charge and he said nothing, but on Tuesday my regular nurse was back on duty and got quite angry with me. She made an appointment with the consultant who, when I saw him, said I should stop. I pleaded with him to let me finish the course as there was now only two days left. Reluctantly, he gave in and I finished on Maundy Thursday. The hair has never grown back on the front of my neck, but it saves me quite a bit of shaving.

We left for the States on the Wednesday after Easter and I had one of the best weeks of my life. I was feeling very well and the fresh air on the warm days gave me the energy to walk the whole course each day. We spent most of the early rounds following a favourite of mine, Nick Faldo. He was doing fairly well but it soon became obvious he was not going to win (he did the following year). The Scot, Sandy Lyle, seemed to have a better chance, so we followed him for his last three holes. He won by one stroke from Mark Calcavecchia, a particularly exciting finish because it was dependent on his making a difficult bunker shot at the last hole.

The competition is highly organised and focused strongly on the spectator. There is plenty of space to enjoy the game and the scenery is marvellous. At that time of year the display of flowers around the course is at its most spectacular. There are more seats in stands, placed where the spectators want to be, than on any other course I have visited. The catering facilities are excellent – the Masters Club Sandwich is American food at its best. The shops sell umbrellas, caps, collapsible seats, books on golf and anything you could possibly be persuaded to buy in their very distinctive colours of olive green and white.

My ticket for the full event was £500. In 1988 this was a high price to pay for a tournament. Tickets are still available only to those who supported the Masters when it first opened. People wishing to dispose of their tickets send them to an auction in California, where John's travel agent had bought them, selling them on as part of a package which included the hotel and travel. This method of purchasing tickets is just one of the many idiosyncrasies that have made the Masters famous.

I had to have checks to see whether the cancer had left my throat completely, and to be sure it had not broken out elsewhere. These commenced six months after the treatment ended and continued at regular intervals, the interval between each check increasing until my next breakout of cancer, which was in the bladder in 1992. My surgeon on this occasion was a Mr Morgan, who operated on me in the Humana Wellington Hospital in St John's Wood, a very pleasant hospital with wonderful views over Lord's cricket ground from the top floor, where my room was. Not that I was able to watch cricket in October. I was only in the hospital for two days and it was decided that I should not be given any further kind of radioactive treatment, so I consider myself very lucky not to have had further cancers.

I did have a difficult time in 2007, however, which began with my suffering a slight stroke on New Year's Day, though it was over in seconds. I believed myself fully recovered and was quite prepared to forget about it, but my wife Fiona was not prepared to forget it and phoned our GP after the holiday. He insisted we visit the Whittington Hospital in Archway, North London. The Whittington kept me in for tests and there I remained for two weeks. One test showed that my short term memory had been affected. Other examinations indicated that my carotid arteries had become very shrivelled and furred up. The shrivelling was an after effect of the radiation I had received for the first cancer, and the furring a result of the heavy smoking of my earlier years. My consultant, Mr Mitchell, explained that these arteries supply blood to the brain and while he was operating on one the other would supply blood to both sides. Each artery had, therefore, to be fixed separately. Moreover, he could not attempt the first operation until at least three months after the stroke and I would need to heal for a further three months before the second operation was attempted. These procedures took the best part of the year and when I went home after the second operation I was wearing a catheter and waiting for a further operation the following spring. Thankfully, I have now returned to excellent health, and I think that you and I, reader, have had our fair share of hospital tales in this book.

CHAPTER 18

Bulgaria

Gerry O'Donovan, a teacher at my school, served in the Royal Air Force during the war and returned to school as head of the French Department when the war ended. He was particularly keen to start taking pupils to France during the summer holidays but was still encountering difficulties so soon after the cessation of hostilities. He almost made it work in 1947 and I put my name down. Unfortunately, at the last moment this failed and we ended up going to Eire. The only part of that trip I can remember was the crossing to and from Wexford. It took all night. The sea was very rough and the cattle in the holds below were moaning loudly. We were on deck where the only shelter on the boat was for the ill and infirm. I am pleased to say that the ferries have improved since then. The next year, after I had left school, Gerry was successful and my brother went with him on a cycle tour to Annecy in the south of France, where Gerry's wife had been born. I think there was one more trip to France before Gerry found that he could offer a less expensive and more enjoyable vacation in Salou on the north-west coast of Spain, based on renting holiday flats and taking enough pupils to fill a hired plane to and from the resort.

Some of the pupils who had been on Gerry's trips found that they could not afford the same kind of holiday from the very few agents who existed at that time. So they persuaded Gerry to open up his holidays to past pupils. These vacations became very popular, particularly when he was bullied into including the girls leaving the local convent. He soon found he was having to hire flats for six weeks on end. The planes were also being used more economically because only the first flight came back empty, and Gerry was thus enabled to make the trips even cheaper for his pupils.

My brother Derek and I both went on several of these holidays. Sometimes we would drive down through France to Salou, stopping off at towns on the way. Many of the Old Boys from other years became very good friends. It was on the beach at Salou that I persuaded Brian Hartigan, my senior, and Michael Bolger, a younger man, to become Serrans.

We would go shopping each morning for fresh bread for breakfast and fillings for our sandwich lunch. Our dinner would be in a restaurant, and our evening entertainment was provided by the free entry we were offered at the bar where Gerry was the lead singer. Attractive in appearance and personality, and with an ability to croon in a flirtatious manner, he became quite a celebratory in the resort, and that added to our enjoyment. The beach and weather were excellent and the cost of the holiday low.

I don't know why he moved the holidays from Spain to Bulgaria. It must have been to do with cost, for by 1967 Spain was no longer an inexpensive holiday destination. The Bulgarians were anxious to bring in currency from travellers from Western Europe, and would certainly have been open to negotiation with Gerry who was still taking large numbers of people.

The Soviet state had developed three holiday resorts on the Black Sea coast. Ours was called 'Sunny Beach'. It comprised, almost entirely, very large hotels and restaurants packed tightly into a strip of land between the coastal road and the beach. Our hotel held several thousand people and had more than one entrance and reception. Meals were not served in the hotels, but in large state restaurants. We paid with food vouchers, included in the cost of the accommodation. These could be used in any restaurant, but as the menus, crockery, cutlery, china, and linen were identical and much of the decoration was similar it really did not matter where you went.

I remember our spending some time trying to order Chicken Kiev because it was the only Russian dish we knew. We had no success until one waiter realised that what we wanted was now called Chicken à la Moscow! Although the food was not very exciting, the evenings in the restaurants were great fun. They all had bands, and it was normal to stay on after dinner, either to dance or just listen to the music. The good and inexpensive local wine, together with the Russian vodka, made it easy to have a good time. There were also casinos for tourists who had Western European currency to spend.

The beaches were excellent, and it was fun to walk along ours to the full-size pirate ship, complete with rigging, which had been designed for children to play on. There were, however, very few children and those we saw were not being allowed to climb the rigging. Most of the climbing was being enjoyed by the adults. Sue Breen, a friend of Carol Wilson, was one of those adults. She was able to climb to the top so fast that those around could only stare in admiration. There were also decorated horse drawn carriages that trotted along the roads between the hotels and restaurants, a more relaxing pursuit than pretending to be a pirate.

Many of the other holiday makers were from the USSR and had travelled by coach in parties from offices or factories. For some of them this was a reward for their approach to work, for others just a holiday. Very few were there as a family or group of friends, a fact which might explain why they all seemed to sunbathe communally. One of them would stand and read from a book, while the rest of the group would stand around him or her in a circle with little paper hats on their noses. As the reader finished a page those in the circle would move one pace in an agreed direction. Thus they would be evenly tanned all over. We tried it once but it did not suit our more individualistic approach to life.

The literature advertising the resort offered a list of religious services one could attend by application to the reception. On the Saturday evening Brian, Michael and I decided we would like to hear mass the next day. Reception explained that it was quite a long way to the church but were vague about the distance. It did not appear they had had many requests for the information, but they offered to arrange a cab for us if we could give them some idea of what time mass was likely to be. We said we would aim for ten o'clock and, to be on the safe side, would leave at about nine.

In the morning the cab was on time, but the driver spoke only Bulgarian. He drove for forty-five kilometres before we reached a town called Burgas, where, it quickly became apparent, he had no idea how to find the church. After we had driven around for a while we spotted a man in a cassock, so we stopped the cab and found that the priest spoke some French. As Michael was proficient in that language, we quickly discovered that he was Russian Orthodox. He explained that while the authorities turned a blind eye to worshippers of his Christian tradition, Catholicism was not tolerated. There was a Catholic church but it was locked up and mass was forbidden. Nevertheless, a Catholic priest lived in the sacristy and he showed us how to get to him. We paid the cab to wait.

The church was in a bad state of repair; most of the windows were broken and poorly boarded up. We found our way round the back to the door of the sacristy and knocked. It was opened by a healthy priest of about sixty years. He spoke some French and when we had introduced ourselves he became very excited. Apart from a lady who was allowed to bring him food and an English professor who had taught at the university some time ago, we were the first people he had spoken to for many years. He thought he was the only Catholic priest living in Bulgaria. He had heard that 'Vatican II' had taken place but that was all he knew. He would very much like to read some literature if we could get it to him. He took us into the church and we became his first congregation for a mass in many years. He found an English version of the lesson for Michael to read; we were quite sure he did not realise that it was an Anglican prayer book he had located. After mass we returned to the sacristy, which was where he lived. He ground us some coffee in an antique mill and we drank it without milk or sugar.

We left saying that we would find a way to get him some books about the Second Vatican Council: I took them in my luggage the following year. It was the year the Boy Scouts had their International Camp in Bulgaria, and about six Catholic priests turned up to concelebrate with the Bulgarian. There were no vestments for them so they said mass in their scout uniforms and shorts. A few Italian lady tourists who had found the church joined the congregation and sang beautifully. All entered via the sacristy, however; the church remained 'closed'.

At the end of this holiday I opted to go on a cruise to Istanbul and back from Burgas. When we got to Burgas the Russian ship on which we were to travel was in the harbour but we were not allowed to board. It was a beautifully sunny day and the English were sunbathing. Most of them were lying out on the low harbour walls, while other nationalities queued at the boarding gangplank. After about an hour, a loudspeaker announced that the cruise would be managed in three languages. Our instructions would be given to us during the meals. The first dinner sitting would be in English; the second, an hour later, in French; and the last, an hour after that, in German. Breakfast would be served at 7.00 am in German, 8.00 in French, and 9.00 in English. We would all disembark at ten o'clock. To aid the execution of this plan the German and French passengers were asked to leave the gangplank and allow the English speakers on first. They called several times for the gangplank to be cleared for the English to board but nobody moved, so they had to start boarding those already there. Having been forced into this situation, they then announced a complete reversal of the programme. The English would be the last to board and to eat. In the morning the German speakers, reluctant to take the early breakfast, especially when they could not go ashore until 10.00, came into the later sittings. Confusion reigned.

When we eventually managed to board, our passports were taken away and replaced with Russian visas. The reason given was in case we should lose them in Istanbul, but I believe it was to stop them being stolen by the crew.

We were given very little time to find our simple four-bunk cabins and unpack before the loudspeaker called us in for the third sitting. Ensconced at our long tables, each seating about sixteen people, we were given details of the excursions in Istanbul and the menus for all the meals to be served on board: two dinners, one lunch and three breakfasts. The language was English but no attempt was made to describe the dishes even though we had to decide what we wanted in advance for the entire cruise. When the food arrived it was placed at the head of the table and passed down to us by our fellow passengers. By the time the food reached me, the more interesting meals had been taken, and I was left to select from a poor remainder. An indication that the crew understood the problem they had created came when at the next meal they served the food from the other end of the table.

It was the first time I had visited Istanbul and it proved to be a marvellous experience,

The following year I returned to Sunny Beach to benefit from the knowledge I had gained during the previous holidays. Although we were not encouraged to leave Sunny Beach it was easy to catch a 'bendy bus' and travel elsewhere. I took one to Burgas for the Sunday mass, where I found the priest had not only opened the front door of his church but was standing there to welcome what had become a small congregation, and the church bell was being rung to greet us. He was a very happy man and a very brave one. I only hope his church was able to remain open for the several years before Catholicism became acceptable to the authorities.

At the end of the holiday I travelled back with the party as far as Burgas and purchased a ticket for a flight to Sophia. Here I found an hotel and spent two days sightseeing with the emphasis on architecture. I was amazed to see how much our buildings owe to advertising. There was no advertising on any of the buildings in the Bulgarian capital. Even the products on sale were without the colourful packaging and labelling that give our shops and high streets their character.

I am not a linguist. It may be that my dyslexia has prevented me from remembering more than a very few words in any language, so I have to rely on my ability to communicate in English. I was, therefore, surprised at how well I managed in Sophia, where I found enough English speaking people to help me. It was a different story, however, when I came to leave. The taxi taking me to the airport was stopped at an army check point, and my driver entered into a long conversation before we were allowed to proceed to the next check point. I then became aware that more military transport than I would have expected was passing us on the road. We halted again when we reached the entrance to the airport, which was guarded by soldiers. Again a lengthy conversation ensued before we were allowed to proceed to the terminal. This was full of anxious people sitting on anything available, but nobody was manning the check-in desk. The woman I spoke to did not understand much English and was only able to tell me that there was no flying today. I could not understand why. Despondently, I found a seat and began thinking about what I should do. I had not long been seated when I realised that the man sitting next to me was reading a book in English. I started a conversation. He was Dutch and told me that the Russians had stopped the movement of all private transport until further notice. I was lucky to have reached the airport.

I considered returning to Sophia but the airport seemed safe enough, so I decided to wait and see what would happen. After a while my Dutch friend put his book down and we began talking about where we lived and what we did for a living. He let slip that he had managed to get on the flight list for a plane carrying press to London that afternoon. I asked him how. At first he was evasive, then he relented and told me how to do it. I went to the desk, showed my ticket, and said I was press. The receptionist recognised the word press and looked at a list of names on a sheet of paper. When it was obvious that she could not find my name I took the sheet and examined the list, whereupon I appeared to lose my temper, cursing and shouting that it was a bureaucratic mistake my name was not there and that she should correct it. "I must get to London," I stormed. "I have urgent business in London." To my surprise she copied the name from my passport onto the list without question.

That evening, thanks to my Dutch friend, I managed to

board the plane and subsequently land in the UK. There I found that everyone knew the Russians had moved troops in to quell an uprising in Czechoslovakia. They had also stopped domestic flights over the entire Soviet Republic. It was August 1968. Had I not been able to leave when I did, I might have had to spend four days in that airport.

CHAPTER 19

Orthodox Jewry

I do not remember who introduced Mr Wolff to our practice, or the circumstances of our first meeting, but I do remember him giving me a Jewish calendar, and making it a condition of our employment that we should not work on any of their commissions after noon on a Friday or on any of their holy days. He told me that he had used a liberal Jewish surveyor in the past but that he had not respected their religious laws. Accordingly, he had made various enquiries and had come to the conclusion that my Catholic practice could solve his problem.

Mr Wolff represented the Wolff Charity Trust, which acted for the Hasidic synagogue in Stamford Hill. We did some minor work in the synagogue but we never met anyone else connected with the Trust or the synagogue. Mr Wolff seemed to be totally responsible for the Trust. He was buying outmoded laundries which we modernised and converted into smaller industrial units. They were easy to find because they all had large water storage tanks on iron framing well above the factory space. One of the first sites we tackled was in Tooting where the tanks were at least twenty feet by sixteen, and eight feet high, perched above the laundry. One Friday lunchtime the contractors were about to leave for the day when they discovered a leak in the tanks. The water was coming down quite fiercely and would drench the whole building by Sunday. What did I want to do about it? There was just enough time for me to telephone Mr Wolff, who decided, irrespective of the potential damage. to leave it. We agreed to meet on Monday to review the resultant mess.

He was just as keen to prevent me working on a Sunday, so our building contracts were based on four and a half days with an extra hour added to the first four days.

A further incident relating to the prohibition of work on the Sabbath occurred during the demolition of another laundry. The District Surveyor had been contacted by members of the public worried about a portion of wall they feared might be about to fall. The District Surveyor decided it should be removed, and contacted me on a Friday afternoon. I could not get in touch with Mr Wolff so I brought builders back to take it down. When I reported to him on the Monday he thankfully agreed that I had been right to obey the law of the land!

I was very impressed by Mr Wolff's strict approach to the spiritual aspects of his religion. He was not only very committed to observing the holy days and periods, he did so with great conviction. One of our commissions was to remove the roof and any branches that might have grown over the shed called a 'sukkah' where Mr Wolff would live under the stars, on his own, for five days during the Festival of Tabernacles (Sukkot).

I was less impressed with the many cultural and dietary conditions he adhered to. He lived in two semi-detached houses joined together. This arrangement enabled the gardens to become one and the garden reception rooms to have the dividing wall removed. The resulting spacious area became the dining room for his family of nine children with a kitchen at either end so that both Kosher and non-Kosher food could be served and we could each have coffee together in the dining room, mine coming from one kitchen and his from the other. When we were out for a day looking for sites he would insist on buying me lunch in a restaurant; while I ate he would sit at the table and take out of his brief case a sandwich and an apple. His appearance was sufficiently unusual for the restaurants to raise no objections to his eating food on their premises which he had not purchased there If, as occasionally happened, his wife was with him she would walk a little distance behind us.

There came a day when there were no more laundries to convert and Mr Wolff started instead to look for run down factory sites to make into smaller units. Several of these lent themselves to the building of extensions and in one case in Hackney I had occasion to explain to Mr Wolff that although I recommended applying for planning consent we did not have to do so. The proposed single story extension would be behind a high wall surrounding the factory yard, and there was a loophole in the law which permitted the interpretation that if you could not see it, it did not exist. He got quite excited and insisted that we should not seek consent. The planning authority never saw the building behind the wall, so my advice was not tested but it was a very brave decision of his.

It was at about this time that I received a telephone call from the chief executive of the London Borough of Hackney asking me whether the Wolff Charity Trust would be interested in working with the Borough to produce small industrial units. I said I would speak to my client but I did not hold much hope. I put the proposal to Wolff in the most glorious terms and he was persuaded to come to a meeting at the Council offices. Although he appeared to listen very thoughtfully, he turned down an offer that any other developer would have leaped at. I wish now I had asked him his reasons – but I don't think he would have told me.

After some time, he started to involve his son Maurice in the business, and, although I thought I was getting on with him, our relationship with the Trust ended when we finished the building work on the last commission Mr Wolff himself had given us. So concluded my association with a most interesting representative of Orthodox Jewry.

CHAPTER 20

Ischia

I have known Leon Manzi for many years, and no longer recall how I met him. We had been at the same school, but he was younger and closer to my brother Derek's age and I don't remember him there. I did know his cousin, Louis Manzi, who eventually took over his father's famous fish restaurant in the West End. He had arranged for an uncle to invite a few of us boarders for tea on Saturdays – a way for the boarders to get out of their house for shopping and the odd trip to the cinema. We also enjoyed playing on the dodgems and slot machines which the uncle repaired in his very large house on the junction at Whetstone, North London. This has now been replaced by a Barclays Bank. I don't remember Leon being there either.

My first memory of him is in the mid-1950s. He took me for spaghetti at his mother's house in a road opposite Hampstead Heath. It was the first time I ate pasta that had not come out of a tin. The whole family of nine was already sitting at a long table when we arrived, and it was obvious that Leon, who was not the eldest, had taken the place of his dead father as head of the family. At that time he was making a living providing 'one arm bandits' for clubs and pubs. He had a minder who carried a gun but the business proved too dangerous, despite the minder, and he gave up slot machines and opened a restaurant called The Armoury in Cannon Street. It was very successful, and closed only when the freeholder sold the site for office development.

It was at about this time that we were preparing to open The Island Queen in Islington, and we invited Leon to open a restaurant on the first floor. This was also a success, and he ran it until John Evans took it over. It was probably during this period that I had the idea of persuading my architect partner to invest in property that would provide the practice with additional work. We persuaded Leon, and Claude Luzzatto also, to put in a thousand pounds, and with two thousand from the practice we purchased a house on Crouch Hill. We let the house until we had amassed enough rent to convert it into flats. Then we sold the flats for enough to purchase and convert another house on Crouch Hill. Thus we had the start of a property company that gave work to the practice.

Over a drink one evening Leon and I were dreaming about our futures and hatched the idea to open a luxury hotel for the most wealthy, on an island in the Mediterranean, one with a good harbour for yachts. A little later that summer Leon read about a piece of land that might be suitable on Ischia, a small island off the Italian coast near Naples. The land was owned by Asti, the wine growing family who produce Spumante. We contacted the agents; they were prepared to finance our visit and arrange for someone to meet us at Rome railway station. The man they sent was an Italian pop singer called Gino Latilla. We found him at the pre-arranged spot in Rome station signing autographs. When we boarded the train it was already as crowded as a London tube in rush hour, but Gino was a big man who forced a route for us down through the standing crowd to the restaurant car. When we arrived it too was crammed full but a member of the restaurant staff recognised Gino and asked for his autograph. While Gino was signing, he explained apologetically that no meals would be served as the train was too full, but we could use the staff compartment adjoining the kitchen. We accepted and sat on a long bench seat facing a table. In the circumstances it was very acceptable, and turned into a positive luxury when the chef entered with a great bowl of spaghetti bolognaise and some plates – a splendid way to pass the time on our journey to Naples.

At Naples we got a taxi to the harbour and caught the hydrofoil to Ischia, my first experience of this exhilarating form of speed on water. The house and the estate were on a cliff at one end of the island, and there was the possibility of access down onto the beach of a sheltered bay. It would certainly have been possible to build a harbour and it would have been ideal for our purpose. I am not sure that we were really serious when we set out on this free weekend but we were now convinced we had a good idea.

I had my first flight in a helicopter on our way back to Naples, and by the time we had reached London we had decided how to raise the money. We were sure that we could secure the help of the Italian Government, who might even provide some cash, and it would certainly attract a spending clientele. Leon spent some time on it when we got back to London, but I am sorry to say that it went the way of many dreams. We lacked the courage. Looking back, had we pursued and realised our dream it would have been the first of many such places around the Mediterranean that now attract palatial yachts and extremely wealthy owners. My regrets for what might have been still surface occasionally.

CHAPTER 21

The President of France

A favourite restaurant of mine is the Hotel L'Atlantic in Wimereux, a small town on the French coast some five miles from Boulogne. It was possible, even with the time difference, to go there for lunch and be back in a day. I used to do this fairly frequently on Sundays during the spring and autumn. The restaurant specialised in fish but one could also order meat and chicken, cooked beautifully on a wall rotisserie. Their most famous dish (a first course) was Terrine de Turbotin and consisted of a long 'box' composed of slices of turbot and filled with an assortment of shellfish in aspic. The 'box' was then cut in slices like a veal and ham pie and served with a sauce based on whole grain mustard. The cut through the terrine gave the shellfish the appearance of exposed fossils. The bar was on the ground floor with access from the esplanade on one side and, on the other, from a side road running parallel to the main road between Boulogne and Calais. The restaurant itself occupied the first floor and had generous windows looking out to sea. The family who owned L'Atlantic had a much larger (and less expensive) restaurant and hotel on the sea front in Boulogne.

My only difficulty with L'Atlantic was the tendency of the staff to be even more pompous than is usual in a good French restaurant. On the occasion I introduced my friend John

Mother and Father

Derek

Age 8 1/2

Sketch Party at Northern Poly

Food Queue

Office outing La Ronde nightclub, to celebrate Ron's marriage.
L-R: GM, Ron Gillings, Mary Gillings, Sonia, Don Steele,
Anne Robbins

Irina, GM and interpreter, Bulgaria

Above left: During the Congress '81, Genoa, Italy, May 17th
Above right: GM outside The Loft
Below: Practice Model Wembley

Above: Meeting Pope John Paul II
Below: Serra Conference, Genoa

Above: Kevin at GM's wedding 2005
Below: Colin Beswick, GM, Reg on the opening night

Above: Stanhope House
Below: Wedding Day

SYNODUS EPISCOPORUM

Secretaria Generalis

A CORONAMENTO DEI LAVORI SINODALI SULLA FORMAZIONE DEI SACERDOTI HO LA GIOIA DI INVIARE L'ESORTAZIONE APOSTOLICA POST-SINODALE «PASTORES DABO VOBIS» DI SUA SANTITÀ GIOVANNI PAOLO II, CON FERVIDI E FRATERNI AUGURI DI BUONA PASQUA!

+ Jean P. Schotte

PREGHIERA DEI FEDELI

Il Maestro delle Celebrazioni Liturgiche Pontificie autorizza il latore del presente a partecipare alla celebrazione presieduta dal Santo Padre.

Vaticano, _____

UFFICIO
DELLE
CELEBRAZIONI
LITURGICHE
DEL
SOMMO PONTEFICE

IL BIGLIETTO DOVRÀ ESSERE PRESENTATO
CON UN DOCUMENTO DI IDENTITÀ
AD OGNI RICHIESTA DEGLI INCARICATI

8° Synod of Bishops

The Rector of the Venerable English College
requests the pleasure of the company of

Mr Gerald Murphy

at   Ven College Inglese

on   Sunday 21st October, 6pm - 7.30p

Ven Collegio Inglese
Via Monserrato, 45
Roma

R.S.V.P. Regrets only
Tel. 657.889.565.808   686.5808

DAL SANTO PADRE

GIOVANNI PAOLO II

A RICORDO

DELL'VIII ASSEMBLEA GENERALE ORDINARIA
DEL SINODO DEI VESCOVI

30 SETTEMBRE - 28 OTTOBRE 1990

Synod invitations

Evans, and his friend Jean, to the restaurant, I had naturally undertaken to pay for the meal but John insisted on paying for the wine. He called upon the services of the sommelier and a very expensive claret was duly chosen. However, it was not the sommelier who brought the wine to the table, but a waiter who proceeded to splash the wine into John's glass so carelessly that a quantity of sediment found its way in as well. On complaining to the sommelier, John was told that in France it was not considered necessary for the sommelier to pour the wine; their waiters were perfectly capable of doing so; the sommelier was there merely to give advice. He also added that it was only in England that the wine was poured gently so as not to disturb the sediment; the French were more patient and allowed the sediment to settle in the glass. As the reader can imagine, my friend was livid. He was sure he was being ridiculed, but not sufficiently sure to dispute what the sommelier had said. However, we did not allow this minor upset to spoil our meal.

I was entertaining Leon, Jenny, and their five year old daughter Zoe to dinner in the same restaurant on the Sunday before one of our Bank Holidays, the intention being to use the Monday to return slowly to England, a good arrangement because it was not a holiday in France. The roads and ferry would, therefore, be less crowded. For the same reason it was easy to reserve two of the four or five rooms at the hotel. Zoe was only five and although her rather delightfully precocious manner provided great entertainment for the others in the dining room, she was getting tired before we had finished dinner and had to be taken upstairs to bed. We remained in the restaurant and it was quite late before we retired for the night. As a result we were late coming down to breakfast. The staff were surprised and embarrassed to see us, as they thought that all the guests had left.

We then learned that the town had been closed by the police and nobody could come in or go out because the President of France was visiting and hosting a lunch at the hotel. We would have to stay there until late afternoon. They did, however, accept that it was their fault we had not been informed and that they should have realised we had not checked out. As recompense, they invited us to be their guests for lunch.

We went for a stroll and, returning at the agreed time, were shown to a table at one end of the restaurant, around which a screen was placed to conceal us from a very much larger long table at the other end of the room. After a short pause we observed the President and his guests enter. Had we spoken better French we would have been able to understand some of the conversation.

We never discovered the reason for the President's visit; I do not think the staff knew. It may have been a state lunch because some of the guests wore military or naval uniforms. We were served with the same courses as those for the President's table. I cannot now remember what we had to eat, but it was impressive and we felt the delay to our journey had been worth it.

CHAPTER 22

Politics

The end of every decade was always a bad time for architects. It heralded an economic downturn and our clients would decide that the time was not right for investing their money. This meant a shortage of work. In the 1960s it came a little early, so in the summer of 1968 I started to think about trying to get a seat on the local council. I wanted to know who decided my planning applications – who exactly were the butcher, baker, and candlestick maker? How did the decision process work? To do this I would need to become a councillor. I asked my secretary, Melody, to get me an appointment with someone in one of those political offices I had seen in the High Streets. She came back with an appointment with a political agent at an address in Tottenham Lane, Crouch End.

Approaching the address, I saw that it was a shop with Conservative Party posters in the window. I hesitated, because I had been a socialist when I was a student and even now I was probably still left of centre. "But," I thought, "I am only seeking information so this is as good a place as any to start." I went in and a smart, elderly gentleman in a light brown tweed suit greeted me from a desk at the far end of an otherwise empty room. I told him I had come to find out how to become a councillor. He introduced himself as a retired army officer who had taken up the role of Conservative agent for the Borough of Haringey. He had not been a councillor himself but he had worked with the council for several years. "I will try and help you," he said. "Name, age, address and occupation, please." He thought that an architect could make an important contribution to several of the council committees. "You will have to go before a selection committee, of course. Are you aware there will be an election next May?" I said I had heard that. He told me that most of the seats were already filled but he could still arrange for me to meet the selection committee. I should not, however, expect to be selected, even for a losing seat, at this election. He completed what appeared to be a form and asked me how long I had been a member of the Party. I admitted that I was not a member. "You'll have to become one before you can be considered, you know, and I must ask you for a subscription." I said I would be happy to join the Party and inquired as to the amount of the subscription. "I am not allowed to ask for a specific figure," he replied, so I offered him ten pounds which he declared to be very generous and signed me up for last year as well as this one. "It will look better on your CV," he explained.

A few weeks later I received a call from a Mrs Perry who introduced herself as the Chair of the Selection Committee, and a meeting was arranged. The committee consisted of four people who asked me a number of questions – mostly about how much effort I was prepared to put into the election campaign. I must have satisfied them because they offered me a seat in Tottenham. This was a Labour stronghold. Within a few days Mrs Perry phoned to say that because one of the other candidates had taken a post abroad, they were now able to offer me the marginal seat of Turnpike Lane. I accepted and was, by the beginning of September, canvassing in what was referred to as the 'ladder', so called because it consisted of roads running parallel to each other between Wightman Road and Green Lanes. I tried to get the other candidate for the ward to help but he was not prepared to canvass for what he thought was a loser. He was probably right because the ward had never previously voted Conservative and the Labour candidates standing against us were senior members of the existing council. I met one of them, Andrew Macintosh, on a couple of evenings after canvassing, when we would have a drink together in the only pub near our ward. He was certainly not expecting to lose his seat. In fact, he went on to win a seat as prospective leader of the Greater London Council and became leader, only to be replaced later by Ken Livingston and given a seat in the House of Lords.

My ward committee was small, but very keen, and they taught me everything about canvassing. They were also very good at recording everything I learned about the people to whom I spoke. This enabled them to make lists of those we thought would vote for us at the forthcoming election, so we knew who to call on polling day.

The secretary was a very efficient ninety-year-old who had won the competition to find the name for the new borough of Haringey, when the original boroughs of Hornsey, Wood Green, and Tottenham were combined to form one larger borough. It had been the name of a local stadium, demolished to make way for a supermarket, and part of the surrounding area when she was young, and was still the name of a passage running between the roads that formed the ladder.

I had visited almost every household in the ward at least once before the election in May 1969, and spent as long with them as they would allow. Conversations were based largely on what I thought they should get from their council and I must admit I painted a rather better picture than the reality. The only knowledge I had was what I had learnt from three meetings for prospective candidates held in the old Council Chamber in Hornsey Town Hall, a much more impressive chamber than the one in the new Wood Green Civic Centre which had replaced it. The sloping floor with its beautiful leather seating, arranged in a semi-circle, gave emphasis to the grand mayoral seat at the focal point of the chamber. I liked sitting in this place of power. It gave me another reason for winning the election, and I was very impressed with the leaders who addressed us there. They were much more accomplished than I had anticipated. They were also much more convinced that we would win than were we who listened to them.

My fellow candidate and the ward committee did come out for several evenings as election day drew nearer, and on the day itself they were exemplary. They had drummed up enough people to man the office, the polling station, do the knocking up and drive the elderly to the polling station. Those at the station took the election number of those voting and this information was matched against our assessment. We were then able to see how we were doing and who we still had to persuade to vote. Towards the end of voting day the streets were full of cars going to and from the polls.

After the polls closed I stayed on in the committee rooms to have a much needed drink and thank the helpers for their contribution. Later, I went to Alexandra Palace for the count. I had seen counts on television, but being involved in one was much more exciting. You can actually see the piles of your votes growing alongside those of your opposition and it certainly looked as if I was winning. It was, nevertheless, a real shock at the end of the counting to find we had achieved a significant majority. That was the only time Conservative Councillors ruled in Haringey. Today there are no Conservatives at all on the council.

The next morning I expected something to happen, but

nothing did. When I had still not received a call by Sunday I felt I should telephone someone. The Leader, Peter Rigby, was the only one I knew socially so I gave him a ring.

He explained that he and a few other senior members were still considering the posts we were to be offered. These would be released before the end of the day. Nothing would happen till the following morning when the various chairs would be contacted by their Chief Officers. Decisions concerning my future had, however, been made and he was able to ask me if I would accept the chair of the Development Control Committee, and Vice-Chair of the Planning Committee. I accepted at once and put the phone down, amazed, thrilled and a bit scared. To find out about the Development Control Committee was why I had gone to see the agent in the first place, and now I was to be its chairman.

I was given this amount of responsibility because there were more chairs to appoint than we had experienced councillors. Many were on the council for the first time. This led to a strange experience. The Development Control Committee was the first to meet and I was surprised to find so many councillors in attendance. After the meeting I asked whether we were expected to attend all the committees and sub-committees, and was told that was not the case. They had, as first time councillors, attended my meeting to see how such committees were chaired, not realising that I myself was one of the new members.

I not only found all I wanted to know about development control, but I was able to bring to the role a very positive approach. I endeavoured, where possible, to give every application I was unhappy with a practical alternative that we could approve. My time on the Planning Committee was also constructive and, under chairman Brian Falk, a fellow architect and also a first time councillor, I was involved in turning a disused railway line into a parkland walk from Highgate at one end of the borough to Tottenham at the other. It is still very popular with the local residents – and with many forms of wildlife.

I soon discovered there were also important social aspects to a councillor's life that I had not expected. Early one Monday morning I received a call from the Civic Centre, asking if I could attend a lunch later that day to celebrate Tottenham Hotspur's winning the European Cup. The team was travelling around Tottenham in an open-topped bus which would stop for a celebratory lunch at the old Tottenham Town hall. It sounded fun and I readily agreed to be there. I still support my father's team, Arsenal, but I could not call myself a real football fan as this story will illustrate. I drove to the Town Hall but found I had to park some distance away, owing to the large crowd of fans around the entrance and adjoining roads. There was no reception and no introductions. We went straight into lunch and I found myself seated between two men I did not recognize. I turned to the man on my right, who seemed to be too old to be a player, and started the conversation by asking him what he had done to get invited. He told me he was one of the most important people present. He arranged the fans' transport for the away matches, and without him European football would fall apart. He booked over seventy coaches for matches abroad. I then turned to the man on my left and asked him what part he played in Spurs' success. He told me he was Martin Chivers and was very surprised that I had had to ask. Not only did he play for Tottenham but he was also in the English team. He was so upset he declined to take part in any further conversation with me, so I left it to the two secretaries from the Civic Centre who were seated on the other side of my neighbours. I never again accepted an invitation to a meal given to celebrate something I did not understand.

There was, however, another occasion when I did accept an invitation to a surprise lunch after I had completed a year on the Council. It came from our leader, Peter Rigby, and was held at Bertorelli's in Soho. There were just the two of us. It was an excellent lunch. We did not 'talk shop' at all – at least, not until after we had finished eating. It was only when the coffee arrived that he announced he needed to discuss some council business. Education was causing a great deal of problems, and occasioning some very bad publicity. We were failing to improve the education of our West Indian children, the banding system we proposed introducing was unacceptable to most parents, and the Hornsey College of Art students had been enjoying a 'sit in' for many months. The Chairman of the Education Committee was being promoted to a position in the American branch of his bank, so there was the opportunity to appoint a new chairman. Would I be prepared to take this on? I questioned the wisdom of appointing someone who was not on the committee, whose only knowledge of education was what he had gained as a school boy, did not have children of his own, and was unmarried. I thought the papers would have a field day. He replied that we had the right policies; all we needed was a more tolerant type of person with the ability to explain our position. The challenge interested and excited me. I agreed. He paid the bill and I took the tube back to Highgate.

When I entered the office, my secretary, endeavouring obviously (and just as obviously failing) to appear calm, asked what I had done. She had received calls requesting me to appear on two television news stations, be a guest on a radio news station, and give numerous interviews to newspapers. Peter must have got back to his office before me. That evening I spent rushing from one TV studio to the next, painfully aware that I should have been given more time to learn about the problems Peter had told them I was going to solve. However, I was to some extent saved by the interviewers' having to explain to their audiences what a particular problem was before asking me how I proposed addressing it. I was also assisted by the fact that they seemed more interested in how someone without the necessary knowledge or experience could handle education than they were in hearing my answers to specific questions. I thoroughly enjoyed it.

In the days that followed I appeared in many national and local papers. On the first weekend I had my picture on the cover of, and an article in, *The Times Colour Supplement*. I also made the centre pages of *The Times Educational Supplement*. These were much more detailed interviews, of course, and I had time beforehand to talk to my officers and think about what I was going to say.

When the excitement of the publicity died down I had to turn my attention to solving the problems. Peter had omitted to tell me about the most difficult one. The vice-chair of the committee was an alderman who had been appointed to give conviction to our policies. He was the headmaster of Highgate School and very capable, but this was a private school, and politics was not his strong point. He was also unable to deal with the press. His answer to the West Indian problem was their vocabulary. He claimed that it was limited and affected their ability to learn. Unsurprisingly, the West Indian community were not prepared put up with that and the press were not kind in their reportage. I used my lack of knowledge as an excuse for not commenting and offered to look into the matter. The problem then died naturally. I took a similar approach to the other issues. By providing a cooling off period, asking for more consultation and being prepared to give a little on the fulfilment of our policies normally satisfied the most difficult. I was also well advised by a splendid team of officers, ably led by Alan Slater. He taught me how officers can be just as helpful when they don't agree with the policies as when they do.

The Hornsey College of Art 'sit in' had begun in the same month as my election. Responsibility for the day to day control of the college was with Shelton, the Principal, and Alderman Laurie Bains, the Chairman of Governors. For nearly two months the students had controlled the college. They provided films, music and meetings instead of classes. Teachers were replaced with speakers like Jack Straw, the President of the National Union of Students, Lord Longford, and Tariq Ali. They wanted Art & Design qualifications to have parity with university degrees and students to have equal authority in decision making with the teaching and administrative staff. Despite a security firm with dogs being employed to secure the building, students managed to enter and leave with apparent ease.

The only time I had direct involvement with the 'sit in' was just after my appointment as Chairman of Education. It was on a fine summer evening in late July. The students had invited a guest speaker, and I was asked to attend. Just before reaching the college I happened to pass an outside broadcast vehicle stationed opposite in Crescent Road. An interviewer recognised me and asked me to comment on the meeting. I told him I did not think it was important and I was surprised he was there. especially since the speaker was not very exciting and most of the students were away from London. I crossed the road and, before entering the college, turned around to find that the TV vehicles were all leaving. I have since realised that a politician gets credit and publicity only for solving problems, not for helping them go away. That was the last major event at the college. Eventually, in July 1970 a compromise was reached. Some students, and teachers were invited onto the governing body and the 'sit in' lost much of its heat. I agreed with the Principal and Chairman to repair the not inconsiderable damage and to use this decision to postpone the opening of the college until November.

During the 'sit in' we had been asked by the Ministry of Education to consider taking the college into the proposed new polytechnic being formed with the Boroughs of Barnet and Enfield, but we avoided discussing this with the college authorities while our attention was focused on the student protest. The matter was postponed until the following year when I became joint Chairman, with Vic Usher from Barnet and Mrs Emsden from Enfield, of the Joint Steering Committee to create the Middlesex Polytechnic, the precursor of Middlesex University.

I have no recollection of the debates that covered most of the issues with Hornsey College of Art being part of a polytechnic, but we managed to resolve most of them by reasonable compromise to the satisfaction of the college and the other two boroughs. The notable exception was the regulation governing the students' attendance. They were to sign a register before 9.00 am and remain in college for the whole day. Failure to do so could result in exclusion from the course. Our college wanted exemption from this regulation, and we were prepared to go along with this. Barnet and Enfield were not. It was decided to add the question to 'any other matters in dispute', to be settled at the end of the process. In the event, it was one of only two matters not resolved prior to our last meeting. The other was the name of the polytechnic. Most of the committee thought that these items would take our last meeting until after midnight and had made arrangements accordingly. I was in the chair and proposed at the start of the meeting that they be left till the end and any names members wished considered be handed to an officer on a piece of paper provided. We then proceeded with the rest of the business. When we reached the disputed items I suggested the question of Hornsey College of Art's exemption from the regulation governing their attendance be referred to arbitration by the Secretary of State. Most of the committee were only too pleased to see the back of the problem and readily agreed. I next suggested we accept as the name for the polytechnic the one that appeared most often on the pieces of paper. Probably helped by the fear of being there all night, no one objected and we approved the name of 'Middlesex Polytechnic'. Accordingly, we adjourned after only two hours and were able to enjoy the reception laid on to celebrate our having produced a constitution.

Later in the year my officers informed me that we had been given a date for the arbitration by the Secretary of State, Margaret Thatcher, but there was a difficulty about the number of officers the three chairs could take with them. Alan Slater, the chief officer, advised me I would need three officers to properly cover the subject and we had been allocated only two. I told Alan to accept the appointment and provide them with the names of the three officers who would be advising me.

When we arrived at the Ministry, Vic Usher (Barnet was Margaret Thatcher's Borough) kissed her on both cheeks and welcomed her with a few personal phrases. She then passed on to Mrs Emsden, whom she also knew personally, and they had a short conversation. When she came to me she said, "You are the one who required more advisers than my officers thought necessary." I explained that our structure required that number to answer the questions which might be asked, adding that I still had less support than those opposing me. She then took her seat in the centre of her officers and asked me to state my case.

I began my presentation with a description of Hornsey

College of Art, emphasising the strength of its reputation and the advantages to be gained by a less rigid structure for students of the arts. I tried to explain why an insistence on signing in before a specific time in the morning, and attendance for the whole day, every day of the term should not be obligatory nor an essential component of their assessment.

When I had finished, Mrs Thatcher rose and without reference to the other parties nor the officers, hers or mine, declared that she agreed with Barnet and Enfield: the standard proposed was reasonable and would be good for the students; I had wasted everyone's time in bringing the matter before her. I replied by saying that as an arbitration the hearing was a disgrace: no consideration had been given to our case, no respect had been shown to me, or the authority I represented; I felt I had been told off by a schoolmistress. She stormed out of the room, looking very angry and left her officers to pick up the pieces. They were kind but could do nothing. We would have to accept the judgement. I should perhaps say that this was very soon after she had been promoted to Secretary of State for Education and she might not have had much experience in arbitration. Nevertheless, she did have a degree in law and should have known better. Naturally, we did not give in on the issue and the polytechnic, sensibly, did not try to execute the regulation for the Art Department.

I encountered Mrs Thatcher again in connection with the polytechnic when we opened an extension in Enfield. I met her at the entrance and showed her around the facility. After the tour she attempted to address the staff and students assembled outside the administrative building, but the students decided to show her that she was not welcome. They booed and yelled to drown her speech. They were successful and she was forced to cut it short. We were then escorted through the crowds to the canteen for tea. As we ascended the steps to the restaurant

I had to stop a student from taking her hat for a souvenir. He managed to remove it from her head but I retrieved it before he could get away. Eventually, we got through the crowd and the canteen doors were unlocked to let us in. The tables were beautifully laid for tea but all the food had somehow already been consumed. The students must certainly have enjoyed that tea, but I expect I lost a few more points.

She never mentioned these incidents at our next meeting, which was at a reception during a Conservative Party Conference. When I was introduced she merely said, "We know each other." I was not to know that Mrs Thatcher would become Prime Minister, or that we would meet many times in the future during my term as constituency chairman. Later, when I became North London European constituency chairman my agent was her agent, and in the run up to the European elections I accompanied her on visits to her own constituency.

Chairmanship of the local and European constituencies involved meeting many important politicians and I remember with affection my encounter with Prime Minister Edward Heath who came to speak to us before a parliamentary election. At the end of the evening the officers of the Association had planned to take him to a pub in the constituency to meet some of the electorate. We had thought it would provide good publicity but Edward Heath did not agree and we ended up drinking malt whisky in my flat – about six of us seated in my rather dimly lit living room. After a while it occurred to me that my elderly mother, who lived in the garden flat below mine, would be very upset if she had not been invited to meet him so I decided to bring her up. I had a key to her flat, let myself in and found her watching television in her dressing gown. When I told her that some friends of mine upstairs would love to see her, she was at first reluctant but eventually agreed to come up. She wanted to change first but I did not know how long my guest would remain upstairs so I persuaded her to come as she was. When she entered the living room her poor sight and the dim lighting made it difficult for her to make out who the people were, and I was able to take her to where Edward Heath was sitting before she had discovered who he was. I said, "Mother, this is your Prime Minister." He was very kind, but she was emotionally bowled over and quite speechless.

I did not realise when I accepted the position of Education Chair that I would be taking on social commitments second only to that of the Mayor. Most schools have carol concerts at Christmas, Passion plays at Easter, speech days in the autumn, parties honouring retiring senior staff and a great variety of other events. I had over one hundred primary schools, and twelve secondary schools, as well as special schools and colleges of further education, all of which believed it would be a good idea to invite the Education Chair to their events. I have managed to visit as many as five schools in an evening at Easter and Christmas.

The compensations for this commitment were the special occasions one attended, like the time I saw the Duke of Edinburgh arrive by helicopter on a very windy day on the corner of a large open space in Enfield. He was there to meet hundreds of recipients of the Duke of Edinburgh Award who were waiting to show him what they had done to achieve it. I had the privilege of being one of a small group of people trying to keep up with him as he moved from exhibit to exhibit. We really did need the time he spent with each pupil to get our breath back. He was particularly generous with the attention he gave to disabled people.

I was also responsible for a careers exhibition at Alexandra Palace. The people on the stands represented every conceivable occupation and were there to answer questions about their work from children at schools in North London. My role was to accompany Princess Anne at the ceremonial opening and tour of the exhibits. Afterwards we were given tea and I had the opportunity to introduce head teachers and those manning the stands to the Princess. In between these introductions we were able to converse, and I particularly remember her saying how difficult it had been for her to listen to the excitement of the other girls in her class discussing their choice of future careers when she had no chance even to influence the career that had been decided for her.

The day chosen for the opening of a primary school in South Hornsey was remarkably wet. The Queen was unusually late and many of those assembled on a platform erected in front of the school were murmuring about how crazy it was to be waiting in the rain for a style of celebration redolent of a bygone age. When, however, the car drew up and Her Majesty got out they all clapped with excitement and the comments that followed were complimentary. My role was to introduce the Queen to the Head Teacher. The Head Teacher then took the two of us around a small classroom exhibition of the children's art. The children stood by their work and were able to talk to her. She was wonderful at getting down to their level and making conversation with them. They did not seem to be overawed, but behaved very naturally. We then went outside to a small area where I had to help Her Majesty lower a small sapling into a prepared hole in the ground to mark the occasion.

My term as Chair ended with the next election. The swing to the Conservatives was not expected to last and I was offered a safer seat in Fortis Green, Muswell Hill. We won this seat but lost control of the council to Labour. (My first seat in Turnpike Lane was lost.) I became Deputy Leader of the party and opposition leader on Education. Many of the members of the committee were the same but instead of taking officers' advice and making propositions one spent one's time rejecting the advice and attacking the propositions. This is particularly difficult for the opposition chair because he or she has to remain on sufficiently good terms with the new chair to be able to discuss the many matters where decisions are required to be made jointly.

I must admit I found political opposition something of a trial. It is against my nature and my professional training to be negative. Everything we do should be constructive and positive. When it was clear that the Conservatives would not obtain control of the council within the foreseeable future, I retired.

CHAPTER 23

Parliamentary Candidate

When I applied in 1972 to be considered as a candidate for the next parliamentary election, I saw myself as a very successful councillor in a borough we had gained from Labour and which had already become well known nationally. Haringey has always enjoyed more than its fair share of media attention and I felt I had a chance of being adopted. In those days members of parliament were not paid; most of them managed to earn a living in a profession. MPs only sat in the afternoon and I felt I could manage the practice and be an active member. I suspect that it was easier then to get onto the 'approved list' because only a few could afford to stand. I had only to attend an interview with the member responsible for compiling the list. This turned out to be a fairly short and informal conversation about my experience and interests; I was not questioned on my knowledge of government or on the matters before parliament. I was found acceptable and started to receive the names of constituencies looking for a candidate. I wrote off to the ones I could manage from London and waited to receive an invitation to be interviewed.

My first invitation came from one of the Coventry seats. I drove up the motorway on a winter's evening in thick fog, which made the venue difficult to find. Fortunately, I had left enough time and was shown into the waiting room before the first candidate was called. I was thus able to study my fellow candidates. We were four altogether, all in the same age group; I was probably the oldest. Some were married; the one that wasn't had a fiancée in tow who looked even more suitably dressed in twin set and pearls than the wives who were present.

I was the last to be called. The chairman, who came to collect me, showed me into a large room filled with some sixty members of the Association and steered me towards two chairs at one end of the stage. "Ah!" he said, looking at the two chairs, "but you are on your own, Mr Murphy." He pushed one of the chairs to the side of the room. If I did not realise at that moment that I had a problem, I certainly did when I attempted to answer the lady members' questions. They were all related to their social events. They were anxious to see how they could replace the wife I did not have. I was not selected. I drove back to London reassuring myself with the thought that travelling up to Coventry every weekend in the winter fog was something to be avoided. After a few weeks, when I had forgotten the fog, I thought that I might have been over conscious of the difficulties for a single man. I still wanted to be an MP. I would try again. My lack of a wife was less obvious in my second attempt. I was interviewed by the officers of the Islington Association who were choosing. This was a more professional meeting altogether and there were no questions that caused concern. I was, however, aware that I could have answered some of the constituency questions more effectively if I had been married and had had my wife next to me. I was not selected.

I am not saying that if I had been an ideal candidate I would have failed. There are examples of single men who have been elected. Sir Edward Heath is one. A single man on his own, however, was at a distinct disadvantage. I decided to give up. But before I had informed Central Office there came news that one of the adjoining constituencies, Wood Green, was looking for a new candidate. This constituency was in our own Borough. I would be known to many of its members and it looked as if I might stand a chance. I put my name forward. I was shortlisted and my interview went well, but I lost to a female councillor whose husband was an officer of the Association.

In retrospect, I have never regretted not being selected. Shortly after I retired from the list, MPs received a salary with a pension and were expected to work full time. The House started sitting in the morning and throughout the day. I would have found this difficult. I have never wanted to give up architecture. I just need a direct connection with the community.

CHAPTER 24

The Catholic Union

I first met Philip Daniel at a reception between an investiture mass of the Knights of the Holy Sepulchre in Southwark Cathedral and lunch at Middle Temple in 1972. He was a retired planning inspector, archivist for the Knights of the Holy Sepulchre and chairman of the Catholic Union Issues Committee. He thought my knowledge as a local councillor and Chairman of Education would be of help to his committee. He asked me to join and I have been a member of the Catholic Union and the Issues Sub-Committee ever since. I became vice-chairman to Philip for some ten years from the late seventies. The committee was later to be renamed the 'Parliamentary and Public Affairs Committee', which goes some way towards describing what it does. A slightly longer definition on the internet states that it promotes a Christian standpoint in public affairs by lobbying both houses of Parliament through submission of papers to government ministers and departments, through the media, through conferences, and public functions. The sub-committee has the backing and influence of the council of the Catholic Union. This has among its membership most Catholic members of both houses of Parliament, plus Catholics from local government, the judiciary, civil service, press, and a good representation of the professions. The present president is Lord Brennan of Bibury.

Our committee of about twenty-five is made up of MPs, local politicians, retired civil servants, professionals from a variety of disciplines, and a representative of the bishops' conference.

Once a year our officers join with the Union officers in a meeting with the executive committee of the bishops' conference in order to discuss our relationship with each other and any particular issues that might be coming up in the future. When I was vice-chairman I went to these meetings; in my day the bishops were represented by Cardinal Hume and Archbishop Warlock. I remember two matters that might amuse the reader on which the Cardinal asked for an opinion. The Cardinal, who was sitting on the Vatican Finance Committee at the time, wanted to know whether we would be happy if he spoke to the Holy Father about how angry the laity felt over the position of the Vatican in the Archbishop Marcinkus affair.★ He himself was upset over the situation and felt that all English Catholics must be equally outraged. He was very surprised when I told him that most of 'his flock' did not share his feelings. They saw it merely as a Chicago bishop getting mixed up with the Italian Mafiosi; they did not view it as a Vatican issue. On another occasion he wanted to know how we would feel about bishops opting out of the National Health Service and having private health care. He had felt strongly that they should stay with the NHS until recently, but now found that a large number of problems which required an episcopal presence in order to be properly addressed could not be solved quickly because the bishop in question might be unable to attend the meeting as he was awaiting an operation on the NHS. An operation with a private health care professional would have been available immediately. It was clear that Cardinal Hume would have welcomed support for opting out of the NHS or he would not have brought the matter up. Archbishop Warlock, however, was very firmly against such action. I attempted to enter the discussion, only to be asked by the Archbishop what knowledge I had of the NHS that qualified me to offer an opinion. I decided I would make a better contribution outside the debate. So did everyone else. So I do not know whether the bishops are in or out of the NHS, but you can see that our problems in the Church were relatively minor in those days.

I often wondered whether the committee was able to justify its existence, but then an issue would arise in a proposed Act of Parliament which threatened our Catholic way of life, and we realised we were essential. More recently, the advance of secularism has created a continuous stream of issues, and we are in no doubt about our role. Matters discussed in recent months have been: assisted suicide, the Liverpool Care pathway as an answer to care of the dying, our right to consider only Catholics for sensitive religious roles, sacred premises being made available for same sex marriages, Catholic schools having to teach pupils about contraception, and the right of our adoption agencies to refuse same sex couples. This last was an older issue which returned as the result of a court having found that the State had no right to stop our agencies refusing to accept same sex parents.

We meet monthly in Portcullis House, where Members of Parliament have their offices, when the House is sitting. Before Portcullis House was built we met in committee rooms adjoining the debating chambers of the House. The new facilities are much more comfortable and, though it is not part of the Palace of Westminster, MPs still join our meetings and we frequently encounter members of both houses in the corridors. Still, it is not the same as being in Parliament itself and feeling part of the legislative process.

When the previous Lord Norfolk was our chairman I would occasionally receive a call asking me to join him in entertaining guests for lunch. He would apologise for our having to be in the Lords' dining room again and make excuses for the food not being as good as it was at his club. Never having been to his club, I could not compare it. The reason he gave for asking me was my ability to keep the conversation going. He felt he needed some help, especially when his guests expected him to be knowledgeable about a particular political issue. Actually, he was very much wiser than he thought, especially on Catholic matters. He was a great defender of our faith in the Lords and a leader of the Catholic laity in the country.

On one occasion a guest at one of these lunches asked if we could have a tour of the House of Lords, and the others present expressed a wish to be included. Lord Norfolk was surprised that his guests had not seen it before. He said he thought we would have come as school children; the place was always full of children. Nevertheless, after the lunch he gave us an unique tour. He followed the route he used for the state opening of Parliament, starting at the base of Victoria Tower where he would await the arrival of the Queen in her gilded coach. He would then formally greet Her Majesty before taking her to the Queen's robing room. Here her ladies in waiting would put on her cloak and crown. He showed us the door between the Queen's and his own robing room. This would be left open so that they could talk while waiting for the procession to start. He would then lead the procession along the Royal Gallery and through the Prince's Chamber into the Lords Chamber. While we were in the latter he told us how much he felt at home in this room. He likened it to our "living rooms where we would keep the photographs of our families on the grand piano." Here he had only to contemplate the armorial shields of the Barons who signed the Magna Carta, displayed in a frieze around the chamber, as he was related to almost all the families of those who had signed that document – a document which became the basis of constitutional government in our country. It is interesting to reflect that this leading layman in our country is a Catholic

★ Marcinkus was the president of the Istituto per le Opere di Religione, The Vatican Bank, from 1971 to 1989. In 1982 he was implicated in various financial scandals which were headline news throughout Europe, particularly the collapse of the Banco Ambrosiano. The Archbishop had been a director of Ambrosiano Overseas, and involved for some years with the bank's chairman, Roberto Calvi, known as 'God's Banker,' who was murdered in June of that year in London.

CHAPTER 25

The Media

I am fascinated to see the growing popularity of house design on television. It ought to be a good opportunity to publicise my profession, but architects are rarely mentioned. There is, however, at least one programme almost certainly centred around an architect, but his profession is not stated. I fear we are not about to achieve celebrity status.

However, I was the architect in a BBC series called 'The Home' or 'House' or something similar, shown in the early sixties. The programmes opened against a backdrop of a model of a typically Victorian suburban house, which I had enjoyed making. The issues discussed ranged from alterations and the permission required for them, to how to deal with rot, infestation and central heating. The programmes also covered associated subjects like door to door salesmen, so I did not appear in every one, although I was in most of them.

They were pre-recorded and between the filming and the presentation my leg was in plaster. Not being able to drive I spent more than my usual amount of time on the tube. I enjoyed watching people looking at me, then at the plaster, and wondering whether I was the person they had seen on television last Sunday or not.

My appearance on television did more for the practice than

anything else we were doing at the time. The same happened when I entered local politics. The interviews I did for the news programmes kept our name before our clients.

These interviews needed a different kind of expertise from that gained doing the programme on the home. I was there because I was on Haringey Council, a body newsworthy in its own right. Items that would not deserve space in another borough become newsworthy in Haringey. I quickly discovered that the topic under consideration needs to be treated in an adversarial fashion. If the subject does not lend itself to such treatment the reporter has to improvise. In this he is assisted by the producer who has constant contact with the reporter by headphone. The use of background film can also be very effective. On one occasion I was questioned on racial problems in Haringey schools: the interviewer asked me if I had come across any instances of white children being bullied by black children. I endeavoured to explain that young children do not distinguish between their contemporaries of different colour or ethnic backgrounds. When I saw a repeat of the item later in the evening I found that this piece of conversation was shown against film of a black boy punching the living daylights out of a white boy. It certainly had not helped me make my point.

When I first took part in a radio interview for the BBC, however, the dynamic was different. I found myself seated at a four foot diameter round table with the interviewer opposite. The microphone hung down between us and I was required to lean forward to speak into it. I think this set up makes it more difficult to create an adversarial situation. The very closeness of the parties makes the interview more friendly. The microphone, table and chairs looked as if they were the same ones used when broadcasting first began – and perhaps they were! I wonder if they are still there.

CHAPTER 26

Allied Irish Banks

The only commission to have resulted from our entry in Yellow Pages came early on a winter's afternoon at the beginning of the 1970s. It was from a man who had just received a dangerous structure notice forbidding him, his wife and three young children from remaining in their home. He had chosen us because we were the first practice with an Irish name working close to his home that he had been able to find under the heading 'Architects'.

Fortunately, I was able to go to the house immediately. The client and his Irish builder were standing outside a Victorian three storey, five bedroomed house. The builder took me inside to see his handiwork. He had, like many builders before him, taken down the wall between the two reception rooms and enlarged the window of the back room facing the garden. This builder, however, had used 4 inch x 2 inch (100 x 50mm) timber to hold up the house above the openings. He admitted that his experience of working on his own was limited, this being only his second project. The first had been smartening up a fish and chip shop by lining the walls with melamine.

I sent the builder off to hire some acrow props, and told him how and where to put them. Then I phoned the District Surveyor and arranged for him to call back as late as he could that afternoon. By the time he returned the builder had enough acrows in place to satisfy the surveyor that the property would be safe enough for the family to return. During the days that followed I managed to show him how to complete the work to the satisfaction of the District Surveyor.

I received no thanks from the client, however. He was too upset by the additional cost of his modernisation, and the amount of my fee. The builder, however, was very grateful. He gave me a bottle of whiskey and thanked me for keeping him out of prison.

The next time I heard from this same builder he had entered into a contract to put some additional bedrooms into an enlarged roof space and found the roof was beginning to collapse. I helped him out of his difficulties, then terminated my involvement by frightening him with a vision of what would happen if I was not in time to save his bacon on a future occasion.

The next time he contacted me by telephone was to ask whether I would like to design a bank. To humour him I agreed. He explained that on the previous evening he had been in a pub on the Holloway Road where he had met a Mr O'Mahony. This very pleasant gentleman was the development Officer for Allied Irish Bank, which was planning to open its first English branch in Kilburn. Mr O'Mahony had found a suitable site, but needed an architect to give him an appraisal in order to get the approval of the Premises Manager in Dublin. I asked the builder what arrangement he had made with O'Mahony. He told me we were to meet him outside Woolworth's in Kilburn High Road at two o'clock next Thursday afternoon, and he hoped I could make it. I asked whether he had a phone number to confirm the arrangement, but this precaution had not occurred to him. I wondered whether I had humoured him enough, but he was such an innocent abroad that I did not feel inclined to let him down.

So the next Thursday I stood outside Woolworth's at the appointed time. Almost as soon as the builder arrived, so, to my astonishment, did Mr O'Mahony. He proved very friendly, thanking me for giving up my time, and together we crossed the road to the shop he had found. It was part of a new shopping development and had much to recommend it as a suitable premises from which to project a new banking image, but there was one very dangerous structural problem. The pot floor between the ground floor and basement car park would have been an easy entry point for burglars, nor would it have supported the weight of the safes. He asked me to put a few notes on a piece of paper so that he could report to the Bank's Premises Manager. I suggested it would be better if I produced a written report for that officer, and he agreed.

My report was answered by Eric Chapman, the Premises Manager, who commissioned me to assist Mr O'Mahony in finding a suitable property and converting it into a bank. This we did and, with Eric Chapman, created the image of the Allied Irish Banks in England. We chose dark green Cornish slate and a hardwood to go with the AIB's corporate colour of dark blue, an appropriate image at that time and much liked by the first customers.

O'Mahony was replaced by Anthony Greeley as the person responsible for developing the bank; he, though Irish, had been brought up in the English banking system. He accepted the challenge and set about finding customers for this new bank. He joined every organisation and visited every place frequented by the Irish, and is reputed to have taken a £1millon deposit from the boot of his car before the first branch was opened.

When we were ready to enter into a contract with the

selected contractor, the staff of the bank in Ireland were on strike, so posting documents to the Head Office in Dublin would have been difficult. Accordingly, it was decided that I should bring them with me on a visit I was making to a family wedding. On the Saturday morning I knocked on a rear door of their head office; it was opened by one of the directors who showed me upstairs and introduced me to two other directors. After we had signed the contracts they invited me to celebrate the event with a glass of whiskey. Finding the whiskey was a matter of moments, but the absence of secretaries meant that it took much longer to locate any glasses. Many months later, at an opening of one of the branches, a director asked me if I had been aware of how embarrassed they had been at the signing of the contract. They had not been told the reason for my visit to Dublin and, believing that in England morning dress was worn by bankers when signing a contract, had felt they were improperly attired.

Another cultural difference nearly caused a little difficulty at the opening party for the first branch at Kilburn. It was held at the Gresham Ballroom in the Holloway Road. The following morning a member of the press rang and asked whether it was true that, as he had heard, the event was run like an Irish Hooley – in a dance hall with bouncers on the door, and spirits drunk from bottles. I was able to convince him that someone had been pulling his leg. It was, however, true that there were bank staff on the door to stop intruders, and there were bottles of spirits and glasses for guests to help themselves. The many other openings I attended were rather more staid in style. But the Bank's early success owed much to this unsophisticated rural Irish approach to life and business. It is a shame they could not have retained more of that character as they became anglicised.

When we were designing the graphics for the first

bank it was decided to call it 'Allied Irish Bank trading as The Provincial Bank of Ireland', since Allied Irish Banks was an amalgamation of several small banks, one of these being the Provincial Bank of Ireland. This had a branch in Throgmorton Avenue in the City and was legally an English bank with full clearing facilities, which enabled it to issue cheques recognised by the other English banks. No foreign bank had ever had these facilities, and the Bank of England had no intention of changing the situation. Foreign banks had offices in England, of course, but with limited facilities; they could not issue cheques. Legally, Allied Irish Banks was now able to join the clearing bank system. The Bank of Ireland, however, challenged this decision. They argued that they were the Government bank of their country, and must be entitled to the same opportunities as Allied Irish Bank. I was not a party to the negotiations but I do know that this opened the door to banks from other countries being given full trading facilities in the UK.

Although the Bank of Ireland started later, they were very competitive and anxious to catch up with Allied Irish. We spent the next ten years racing to open branches before them in all the Irish conclaves throughout England and Scotland. During that time we designed thirty-two branches, plus the many enlargements required to cover the rapid expansion. We also designed the first Allied Irish finance office, and the first money market branch.

Leicester furnishes a typical example of this competitive race. On one of Eric Chapman's many trips to England to attend openings and look for suitable sites, we learned that our rival, the Bank of Ireland, had purchased an existing bank in that city and had only to make alterations and apply a facelift before opening. However, they had not yet started this work. We returned to an estate agent we had contacted before in Lecicester and declared our interest in a new building on his books. That evening we were attending the opening of a branch in Coventry and took the opportunity to speak to the chief executive and Directors about the situation, whereupon we received their consent to enter into the lease and put a contractor on site. I immediately telephoned a contractor who was prepared to send a senior director the next day who booked into a local hotel for the length of the contract, which was to turn this new empty shell into a bank for completion in one calendar month.

The main problem proved to be cutting a substantial hole in the ground floor concrete to enable the vaults to be lowered into the basement. Cutting the slab required a great deal of water and it took a long time for the blowers to dry it out. We did, however, complete on time and the AIB branch duly opened for business at the end of the month. The Bank of Ireland had not finished the facelift on their premises and must have been surprised and not a little upset to hear about our opening.

It was very motivating for the practice to be working for a new business that was proving so successful, and this was reflected in our relationship with the bank's personnel, which was very friendly; we were not only invited to the opening of the new branches, but to other festivities. I remember a great party given for the branch managers and upper management at a hotel near Lords Cricket Ground. The only other guests were myself and the English solicitor acting for the bank at that time. We arrived at the end of a managers' meeting and joined them in the bar for a couple of large shorts before going into lunch. I cannot remember what we had to eat, but in between every two place settings was a bottle of white, a bottle of red, and a bottle of brandy, so no one would go short of alcoholic refreshment. What was truly astonishing was that several of the managers left after lunch for drinks in a local pub!

One day, towards the end of our commission in the late seventies, I was paying my monthly visit to Gerry O'Mahoney, the General Manager in England. We would start at his desk with my telling him and his deputy, David Petrie, how the various contracts were proceeding. Then we would adjourn to a more casual part of his office around a coffee table. Here we would have a drink before going up to the top floor for an excellent lunch in the executive dining room.

On this particular occasion, after we were offered a drink, Gerry asked how the practice was doing. He thought we must be flourishing with all the work AIB had given us. I agreed and told him about the site in Highgate Village we would like to purchase for our new offices. He knew Highgate and thought it would be a valuable site. We told him the price and the size of the offices we could build on it, and he opined that it was a good deal and, as the country was currently suffering a recession, the right time to buy it. He also thought the Bank could lend us the money. I could not get back to the office quick enough to tell everyone my news. I also called our local AIB Manager and, exaggerating a little, informed him we had secured a loan from the general manager. He said that that was impossible because even the General Manager would have to go to Ireland for approval – but he must have called Gerry because the following day he confirmed the loan.

We purchased the site with planning consent for £110,000. Although we were shortly to lose the contract with AIB, we really were very well rewarded for the work we had done, and I continue at Stanhope House to enjoy the proceeds.

CHAPTER 27

The Cardinals

His Eminence, Cardinal John Carmel Heenan thought Serra should be called the Thomas More Society, and that we should convince the Americans to change the name. Nevertheless, he agreed with our objectives and when we were chartered he became our patron. He was very supportive in regularly presenting the altar servers' awards, the prizes for the school children's competitions, and the pilgrim's scrolls to university students. This last task was performed when they were dressed as Chaucer's pilgrims, about to set off on a three day walk to Canterbury.

He was always available to advise us on the kind of activities in which we should become involved, and one afternoon I visited him to seek his opinion on an idea we had for involving university students. We proposed to invite all the students living in Westminster to a meeting in Cathedral Hall to discuss 'The Place of the Church in Modern Society'. We wanted the Cardinal to be present. Our plan was that a discussion on the subject would be started by seminarians, sitting in a circle. Any seminarian wanting to say something would stand in the centre to address his fellows. The student guests would be invited to join the meeting some time after the discussion had commenced. They would be able to take a chair from around the hall and contribute to the argument. Once the discussion was well under way, we wanted the Cardinal to come down the steps into the hall from Archbishop's House, and sit and listen. We would leave it to him to decide when to join in and what he might want to say.

We were quite sure that students in the late 1960s would be very keen to take advantage of an opportunity to tell the Cardinal Heenan what kind of Church they wanted to serve. We hoped this would lead to some follow up seminars which might result in finding students with a vocation to priesthood. The Cardinal allowed us to go ahead but felt sure we would attract only very pious female students.

The seminarians were better than we expected and began a very lively discussion. There were those who thought that the Church was doing a good job, and that it had a positive approach to the growth which followed the Second Vatican Council. Others thought we were not doing nearly enough to help the developing world. When the students arrived the discussion became more heated. The number attending was far greater than we had anticipated and the hall was quickly filled. The Cardinal came in earlier than expected and was able to hear several students giving their opinion as to what the Church could do to improve the lives of people in the third world, with emphasis on what the bishops ought to do to influence the Government. Just as one girl was expressing her views strongly, His Eminence decided to move into the centre. The other students waiting to have their chance to speak gave way to him. He told them calmly and at some length that they had insufficient knowledge or experience to understand the problems they were discussing. They should be more prepared to support and understand what their leaders in the Church and in society were doing to resolve these very difficult problems. He then turned to leave. There was complete silence. However, just before he left the hall the girl who had spoken earlier returned to the centre and said, "Now you know what I meant when I said the bishops were ineffective and inept." There was uproar as the Cardinal closed the door behind him. The rest of the afternoon was rather negative, though the students did eventually agree to attend a seminar led by the Church's choice of spokespersons.

Early the next morning I received a phone call from Cardinal Heenan. He told me he thought the event had been "dreadful" and "very destructive". It was "without any possible positive future". Under no circumstances should we take the idea any further. But by our next meeting, although still rather upset, he was prepared to say that he had learnt something about how and why we were losing some of our brightest youngsters. The next event we asked him to sponsor was a meeting of head teachers to hear three excellent speakers tell them how to create a respect for the concept of vocation in their schools. This he considered very successful.

Serra's relationship with Cardinal Hume continued along similar lines and he was always available to help with our schemes. One very popular scheme he took part in was the introduction of altar servers to different aspects of the Church on a series of Sunday afternoons. They played football against the John of God Brothers' youths with learning difficulties; visited the Mission to Seafarers, College Hill; experienced an enclosed Order at Tyburn Convent, Hyde Park Place; were interviewed on priesthood at the Hatch End Communication Centre; had tea with the Seminarians at Allen Hall Seminary, Westminster; visited the Cardinal Hume Centre, or took tours of the cathedral and Archbishop's House where they would have tea with the Cardinal.

One Friday evening I was leaving Archbishop's House after a meeting with him about Serra and, to make conversation as he showed us out, I asked what he had thought about the new cathedral in Brentwood where he had presided that week at its dedication liturgy. I was chairman of the Brentwood Diocesan Art and Architecture sub-committee at the time. The Cardinal hesitated before explaining that, since the event was being televised, his mind had been focused on his homily and what he was required to do. Then, after another pause, he said, "We had to wait outside the church in procession before the opening hymn." I explained that there was no narthex. After another pause he said, "That was a very large Bishop's chair. Is that where a priest would sit when saying mass." I replied, "No. There is another smaller chair in front of the one you were sitting in." "Is that a good idea?" he asked. "I think there should be only one chair." I paused for a moment before replying, "That is a strange thing for you to say, Your Eminence. You are reputed to have refused some very important people the use of your chair. However, you also have a second chair for everyone else who celebrates in your cathedral." He smiled. "I will have to think about that," he murmured. He was the most modest of men but very conscious of his need to promote and safeguard the importance of the role of Archbishop of Westminster. Two other examples are worthy of note.

Mother Xavier was anxious to have some work we had designed in the chapel at Tyburn Convent opened by a member of the Royal Family and Cardinal Hume. After much negotiation with Buckingham Palace we were given leave to have the Duchess of Kent to open the chapel and, separately, Cardinal Hume to bless it. There is today in Tyburn Convent chapel a plaque to commemorate the opening and a second plaque on the same wall to commemorate the Blessing. On the morning of the occasion, we and the contractors were told to arrive and wait in one corner of the non-enclosure area adjoining the chapel. When we arrived the nuns were already in the chapel, their lay trustees in another corner of the waiting area and the clergy and altar servers in the sacristy corner. A little after our arrival His Eminence arrived and joined the clergy. A little later, as directed by protocol, the Duchess of Kent appeared and was taken into the chapel. After about twenty minutes the Cardinal started to pace up and down in obvious perturbation. After another five minutes he came over and, taking me to one side, asked, "Gerald, do you know what is happening?" I admitted that I didn't and that there did not seem to be anything we could do about it. He said, "I think you should go into the chapel and see what is going on." He was clearly upset. Fortunately, at that point the chapel door opened and Mother General came out to announce that we were about to begin. I never did hear why the Duchess of Kent had been so long with the nuns. Shortly afterwards, she was received into the Church of Rome.

The other example was perhaps more obvious. The interviewers of candidates for the priesthood had decided to have a series of meetings with experts who might help them in their role. The Cardinal wished to be involved whenever his programme allowed. On this occasion we were to discuss with Jack Dominion aspects of homosexuality in the priesthood, and were waiting in the library at Archbishop's House for Jack to arrive. He was already rather late when we received a message apologising for the delay. Apparently, he was still at a meeting at 10 Downing Street. The Cardinal had been annoyed at having to wait for Jack Dominion, but his irritation became much more pronounced when he heard the excuse. When, quite a bit later, Jack eventually appeared nothing was said and the Cardinal behaved as if nothing had happened. At the end of the talk we had questions, and after our questions on the subject had been asked the Cardinal came in with, "Can you tell me why some of my priests, whom I normally get on well with, can get quite angry with me on the telephone?" Jack explained that the anger was directed against the authority Cardinal Hume represented and not against his person: "When they are not actually with you it is easier for them to concentrate on the authority you represent." The Cardinal admitted, "Yes I do have some difficulty in separating myself from my role."

When Cardinal Basil Hume died, I was given the chance to stand guard with the Knights of St Gregory on the catafalque during his lying in state. I was also present at the funeral itself. These were ideal occasions to meditate on his personality and realise how important my knowing him had been for my spiritual life. He really was a truly great man.

The National Council of Serra covers England, Wales and Scotland so we have two patrons. Cardinal Winning, Archbishop of Glasgow, was one of our patrons for most of my active life in Serra. He was very supportive of our work and prepared to attend all our national events, even some of the ones we held in England. He attended the International Serra Convention in Rome and when the Scots were given the opportunity to hold the International Convention in Glasgow he came with us to the previous convention in the USA. He wanted to study his role. He became quite a talking point as the only cardinal the Americans had met who wore no token of his position other than his bishop's ring. He was also to be found in queues with the rest of us. Prior to the Glasgow convention we submitted the Cardinal's name for the award to bishops who had given the most support for Serra, and I had the great pleasure of handing him a cheque for a thousand pounds at one of the sessions of that convention – an opportunity to thank him publicly for all he was doing for Serra.

At a particular Serra National Convention the Cardinal was able to be present only for the banquet, but stayed on to join us in the bar. We were on bench seating in alcove bays around the student bar and he was moving around the bays, talking to the groups present. Eventually, he moved into the bay next to ours, where the members of a new club from The Cotswolds were sitting. They would not have known him. One of their number, an ex-pilot officer with a voice that carried very well, was asking him rather patronising questions about what it was like to be a priest. "Father, you look quite young. Have they made you a parish priest yet?" "Not yet," replied the Cardinal, aware that others were listening, and playing along with the charade. He answered all the questions correctly without giving them a clue as to his real position in the Church. This caused considerable mirth and The Cotswolds group soon realised their error. The following morning, at the end of the business meeting and under 'any other business', Gerard Humphries, the Judge, recalled the incident in some very good poetry. This renewed the laughter of the previous night and made an excellent end to the conference.

I had to leave early from the National conference that followed my election to the post of International President of Serra when, as I was going, I heard the Cardinal calling after me. He had left his lunch and was pursuing me. When he caught up he said, "I have to say that I would have preferred a Scot to have been elected. They would have made a better job of it, but if that was not possible I could not think of anyone who would do it better. Congratulations!" He took my hand and shook it warmly before returning to his meal. He could have mentioned this at any time that morning but he chose to do it when we were on our own. It was certainly much more personal.

I knew Cardinal Cormac Murphy O'Connor before he came to the Diocese of Westminster, when he was Bishop of Arundel & Brighton. I was chairman of the management committee for the Sion House Residential Centre for Religious and secular priests at Angmering. Bishop Cormac made himself readily available and visited the house many times – so often that on one occasion he turned up to open an extension to the house I had designed and asked what he was there for that afternoon. He was very laid back in those days, before he took on the great responsibilities of Westminster.

I also met him when he was chairman of the competition judges for a new Deanery complex at Weybridge. We had difficulty with our scheme because it did not appeal to the parish priest who would be living there. The absence of a garden was one of his complaints. It was also too contemporary for him, but I got the impression that Bishop Cormac liked it.

At the time of writing this chapter our new Archbishop has not been appointed to the College of Cardinals, but it seems appropriate to include him here with his predecessors. I have known Archbishop Vincent Nichols since he was the bishops' representative on the Issues Committee. We also served together with Sir Hugh Rossi on a three man committee to advise the Cardinal on ecclesiastical titles, papal decorations and other similar matters emanating from the Catholic Emancipation Act.

The London Serra invited him, as Bishop in North London, to a dinner meeting. Because Bernard France lived in Hendon, where the Bishop also lived, he was asked to choose the restaurant. His choice was the Hendon Hall Hotel but we considered this too proper for a new young bishop, and decided he might prefer the Two Brothers Fish Restaurant in Finchley Central, run by my friends, the Manzi brothers. At least we knew the food would be good. Serra was represented by Bernard France, Peter Wurr, Chris Hannington and myself. Leon had reserved one of the tables in the window to the right of the door, which was set a little away from the main body of the restaurant. Shortly after we had all arrived and were studying the menu, a girl who had been a barmaid in my local pub noticed me and came over to the table for a chat. She was young and attractive, had a cockney accent and a great sense of cockney humour. As it was obviously not going to be a short conversation I found a gap to introduce her to my fellow diners. I admit to wanting to see her reaction to being introduced to the bishop. (She was lapsed, but still proudly catholic). When I introduced her she paused, unsure how to react, then burst out with, "Gawd you aren't arf young for a bishop – and attractive. I could fall for you. Gerald knows I am lapsed but when I asked him to try and get a ticket for the Pope's visit to Wembley he got me a ticket on the pitch. I wanted to receive the communion but I was eating ice-cream at the time." I then introduced her to Bunny. "Are you Bernard France & Sons, the undertakers?" she asked. Bunny said, "Yes", and she feigned annoyance. "Bishop, you should do something about this man. He buried my catholic aunt and it was dreadful. He charged overtime for working on the Sunday and the coffin was a disgrace. It was not properly finished. I wiped my hand on the lid and the splinters came off in me 'ands." It was embarassingly funny and we all laughed it off. Having nothing to say to Peter and Chris, she hugged and kissed me on both cheeks and went off to join her husband. As we left the restaurant, Bishop Vincent went across to their table to say goodbye personally.

Archbishop Vincent was also the chairman of the organising committee for the National Catholic Jubilee 2000 mass in the Birmingham Arena. I was the architect responsible for converting the arena for the mass and he was very gracious in his thanks for what I had managed to achieve.

CHAPTER 28

Monasteries

The first monastery I became associated with was the one where I returned to my faith, Allington Castle near Maidstone. This was a real stone castle with castellations and a moat. It had been created out of a manor house in 1281 and purchased by the Carmelite Friars in 1952 for a retreat centre. They had made it very comfortable for groups of some fifteen to twenty people. The chapel, dining area and lounge were all furnished beautifully, in keeping with the stone castle surroundings. The bedrooms were less comfortable, but adequate.

The retreat was a great success. My fellow guests were an interesting group of people who got on well with each other. The talks were about art and religion, and enabled me to see for the first time a direct relationship between my work and the faith.

The weekend had the added interest of my seeing a young non-catholic lad of about twenty living as a hermit under the staircase. He had managed to persuade the Carmelites to let him undertake a forty day Lenten fast. The monks had agreed on the undrstanding that he submitted to the Order's doctor, who required only that he take sufficient water. I learnt later that he made the full forty days and was fit enough to enjoy the party they put on for him to celebrate the completion –

even if he did have to be careful about his intake of food and drink! He never told anyone the reason for the fast, only that he was not the beneficiary of his intentions.

The reason I was able to monitor the situation with the hermit was that I made several subsequent visits to Allington. I had been commissioned by the administrator, Father Malachy, to help him increase the capacity of the accommodation. The order employed two Spanish stonemasons who were given full board and some money. Most of this they saved to take home to their families during extended holidays. The stone required was taken from the supply in a field adjoining the castle. When I saw the amount I told Father Malachy that there would not be enough, but he said I should not worry: God would provide. It was only later that I learned that contractors in the area were dumping stone in the field from their demolition work. God may have had a hand in that; he moves in mysterious ways. It was certainly very good to work with stonemasons so skilled and committed to their work, and I particularly enjoyed being foreman as well as architect.

Before the additional accommodation was complete my existence was noted by Father Brennan, the Prior at Aylesford, another Carmelite monastery. I was asked to advise him on difficulties they were experiencing with a building down by the river at 'The Friars' at Aylesford. I resolved this problem and later made major alterations to the community area, constructed a new pottery, created a conference centre and improved the residential accommodation. Virtually all this work was carried out by their stonemasons, which had a special attraction for me as I could experiment, and even change my mind. It was also my only site work. My role in the practice was limited to design and client liaison. I became involved at Aylesford for some twenty years, before a newly elected prior decided to commission a young local architect in preference to a larger firm from London.

I introduced many friends to The Friars. It has a happy, friendly atmosphere, set in beautiful rural surroundings and with some very attractive buildings dating back to the thirteenth century. There is much to see, to buy, and to eat. One particularly appealing feature is The Pottery, designed to allow visitors to see the potters at work. The day ends with a procession, everyone holding candles whilst praying and singing the stations of the cross. The stations depict the events of our Lord's last hours; they are constructed of pottery and fixed to the walls around the gardens and buildings of the monastery.

One of the friends I introduced to Aylesford was Gillian. She was not a catholic, but had been educated in a convent. We were on our way back from a weekend in France. I was due to make a site visit to the Friars during the coming week, and it occurred to me that if we could pop in on the Sunday evening the short detour involved would save me the best part of a day in the week. Gillian was a bit nervous but accepted the idea. It was still light and quite warm when we pulled into the car park and she was surprised at the number of cars and the hundreds of people. We parked and examined the building work I had come to see. On the way back to the car, one of the friars who was talking to visitors, came across and told me that Father Brennan's back was giving him trouble again. I asked if he was receiving visitors and he said that he was sure he would be pleased to see me. He suggested I go to the reception in the community block. We did this and while the young friar on reception disappeared to check with the Prior, I took Gillian into the waiting room and explained that she would have to wait while I went up to his room. She was quite happy to escape from the meeting. This was the first experience of the church she had had since her school days and it was very different. The relationship between the people and the friars was so friendly. After a short while the friar returned to report that the Prior was pleased we had called. He would like to see us. As I started to leave, the friar said, "You can both go up. In fact it is your companion he particularly wants to see. He wants to see what you've found." We went up to his bedroom on the first floor and gathered around his bed. This large, jovial man was dressed in his pyjamas and propped up on pillows. I introduced a very nervous Gillian and after a few pleasantries the Prior said: "As this is a special occasion, we should have a drink." Gillian would normally have asked for a gin & tonic but she found it difficult to say anything. Father Brennan, in an attempt to resolve her embarrassment, suggested we all had the drink of the house, a 'Blessed Trinity'. Nobody objected and the young friar went off to get the drinks. He did not mention that a Blessed Trinity was composed of one part gin, one part sweet vermouth and one part dry vermouth. When he returned and handed us the drinks I watched Gillian. Not realising how powerful it was, she took a large sip and the expression on her face was one of frightened disbelief. The rest of the meeting dealt with my commission, but still gave Father Brennan the opportunity to ask Gillian several questions, based on his misconception that we were in a serious relationship. I could feel Gillian's discomfort and made the excuse of having to get back to London before dark.

One of the friars at Aylesford, who had been appointed parish priest at Walworth, asked me to reorder the church there. It had a long nave with a flight of some eight risers up to the sanctuary. This had a small apse on the left side containing a statue of a seated St Peter. It was common practice for members of the congregation to climb the steps before mass and kiss the knee of the statue. When we reordered the church we moved the tabernacle into the apse and the statue into an extension of the nave at the back of the church, which caused some concern with parishioners who thought we should not have moved the statue. Some felt it belittled St Peter, while others saw it merely as a change for change's sake. On the evening of the reordering special transport was laid on for the elderly, and among those invited was a lady in her late nineties. She told me she was pleased we had put St Peter back where he used to be. I often use this story to help me counter opposition to changes in other religious buildings. Many people are against any alteration to their physical surroundings, not realising that in most cases these would have been subject to many changes throughout the course of their existence.

Very shortly after I had started to work at Aylesford, in the early 1970s, Brian Hartigan, a fellow Serran, persuaded the London Serrans to go to Mount Saint Bernard Abbey in Leicestershire for an annual retreat; we have done so ever since. The Abbey is a Cistercian monastery designed by Pugin in 1840 and completed by others in 1939. It is an impressive group of buildings around a church, the tower of which can be seen for miles from the Charnwood forest in which it is situated.

Whereas The Friars is a happy, cheerful, and spiritual place, well planted in our world, Mount Saint Bernard is a focus of peace and tranquillity where you feel you can pray somewhere outside our world.

We were made most welcome by the monks, and the Abbot, Father Cyril Bunce, hearing that I was an architect, came into the guest house to seek my advice. This resulted in my being commissioned to prepare designs for the alterations necessitated by the liturgical changes of Vatican II. They gave me a copy of a twenty-two page survey of the alterations the community wanted and the number of monks who were in favour of each change. There were many changes which enjoyed a majority of support, but there were differences of opinion as to how some of these changes should be implemented. The various solutions advanced were also listed with the degree of support each one enjoyed. The most detailed was the reordering of the church.

The decision to employ me must have been announced at the monks' chapter meeting on our first evening because from then on I was unable to spend time in the retreat. I was besieged by members of the community taking advantage of the Abbot's permission to tell me their ideas on various aspects of the proposed work. They would find out from the Guest Master when I was in the lounge, or alone in my room, and come over to the guest house to see me.

I was particularly happy with the ideas of Father Bede, the liturgist, and returned to London to produce a scheme. When I took our ideas back to the community there were two areas in which we failed to get majority support. One was our wish to lower the sanctuary floor to the level of the surrounding church – and it has still not been lowered. The second was the position of the tabernacle. We proposed that the sanctuary be in the centre of the church under the main tower and the altar in the middle of the sanctuary. We wanted the tabernacle replaced by a hanging pyx, which could be seen by worshippers on the three sides of the sanctuary. One of those against the idea was Father Alban. This was unfortunate as we depended on him to make the pyx. While we were still discussing the subject, his fascination with constructing the pyx led him to make one. He then wanted to see it work and organised the hanging of it from the top of the tower. Everyone liked it, and it is still there today. It rests some five feet above the altar, and is electrically lowered onto the altar for communion.

As it is the Community's rule never to make a decision in under twenty-four hours following discussion, I spent several nights in the monastery. My availability to the lobbying that occurred during the interval between discussion and decision was thus extended. I enjoyed these visits from the monks to my room because they were always one at a time, which enabled me to get to know them as individuals.

My knowledge of them was further improved when I became the only guest in an otherwise closed guest house. They were using the guest house refectory while their own was being redecorated, so I had to learn to eat with them. This was not easy because they had not changed their custom for centuries. They do not speak during meals: I had, therefore, to learn their sign language. Whenever I made a sign incorrectly, someone would strike my arm – I learned quickly! The practices at mealtimes had developed in order to prevent viruses spreading through the community. Some monks still had their own personal wooden spoons and forks. Newer members had metallic versions and everyone had his own bowl and mug, produced in the pottery. Together with a very large napkin, these were laid in a place allotted to them on the table between meals. Little luxuries, consisting of the odd sweet or piece of fruit, which I presumed had been given by visitors, were often lined up where we would normally have our desert cutlery. When we entered the refectory we cut ourselves bread from a loaf on a side board and placed it next to the fruit and sweets. After grace was said, one of the Community began to read aloud, while the rest of us sat down to eat. We would spread one third of the napkin on the table in front of us, allowing the remainder to hang over the edge of the table down onto our lap and up our front to be tucked into our collars. The bread, bowl and mug would be placed on the napkin. Soup was served in the bowl and milk poured into the mug. When the soup was three quarters finished the remainder became the gravy for the vegetables which were then added to the bowl, the Community being vegetarian except on special occasions. After we had drunk the milk, our mugs would be filled with water, and some of this was used to rinse the bowl before it was filled with cooked fruit for dessert. When we had finished eating, the spoon and fork were washed in the bowl with water from the mug. The napkin was carefully removed and the breadcrumbs eased into the bowl. The bowl was washed with the last of the water, which was then drunk with the breadcrumbs. The napkin was used to dry the washed items, and everything returned to its place.

Knowing and working with religious communities has a strengthening effect on my spiritual life which, with the time I have spent drawing and thinking about the work they have commissioned, has made it easy for me to be a practising catholic.

One of several strong attachments I have made is to Brother Paul, who is responsible for the building and maintenance work at Mount Saint Bernard. Sometimes he has novices working with him but for most of my time there, he has carried out the building work single handed. There is no trade he does not undertake, and no difficulty he does not overcome. He is now past retirement age but he still maintains all the roofs with little or no scaffolding.

His special gifts were illustrated during work on the Octagonal Chapter house. We were turning it into a library as well as retaining its suitability for its original purpose as the chamber where formal meetings of the Community are held. To maximise the amount of shelf space I designed a gallery at first floor level with staircase access. To improve the lighting I proposed that we added some large Velux roof lights. These are made in Scandinavia where they have had experience of keeping water out under most difficult conditions, even when the roofs are covered with snow. They were much more than just timber windows. They had an arrangement of seals that ensured they were weather-tight. Brother Paul felt challenged. He was certain he could make a window that would be just as good. Because of the importance of getting a water-tight roof for a library, however, and because I had never come across an English version that worked, I insisted on the purchase of Velux windows.

I did not do site visits very often because of Brother Paul's reliability. I tended to go only when he wanted to discuss a problem with me. It had thus been some time since I had visited the Abbey when I suddenly received a call from the Bursar, Father Peter. He suggested it would be a good idea if I visited the Chapter House. When I arrived Father Peter walked around the building with me and Brother Paul. This was so unusual that I was particularly careful in examining everything that Brother Paul had done. I closely examined the two Velux windows lying on the floor but they seemed fine. I was about to leave when Father Peter called me back and asked me if I was happy with the windows. I had a further look and asked Brother Paul if they were Velux. He said that one was, while the other he had made himself. I had, in the interests of the monastery to decide on the Velux, but I must admit that I was unable to tell the difference. Whenever I visit the Chapter House now, I find it difficult not to look up at the roof lights and wonder whose windows I am looking at.

I have only recently introduced my wife, Fiona, to Mount Saint Bernard's Abbey. It is an extra blessing to be able to share my influences with her. We took a drive to the monastery to see Father Mark and his newly completed enlargement of the book shop. He was very pleased with the result and is anxious to make it even larger.

I cannot remember how I got to know Father Paul

Brenninkmeyer of the Benedictines at Worth or how he found the practice, but he commissioned us to adapt an existing 1874 Church of England church and vicarage into an ecumenical downtown monastery, in order to provide a centre for a liturgy that would be attractive to young people of different faiths and of no faith at all – a centre where they could stay without making a long term commitment. We produced some very interesting designs for the church based on advanced liturgical thinking. The height was used to create balconies with rooms over the side aisles, a little like a modern version of the Cathedral at Santiago de Compostela. While we were working on the scheme Father Paul moved into the vicarage with catholic and non-catholic volunteers. They recited the divine office in the west end of the church and created a form of monastic life in the vicarage. There were forms of joint worship where the participants separated only for the canon of the mass. These 'services' were very well attended by members of other churches and those who belonged to no church.

I was not surprised when the Worth Abbey community were involved in a series of television programmes which showed young men spending a few weeks in a working monastery, having an experience of monastic life. They have proved their interest in influencing the society around them.

I have also learned much from female religious communities. I particularly admire the Carmelites, and I enjoyed providing work rooms and guest accommodation for Sister Paula at the Walsingham Convent in Holt. I was fascinated to learn how icons are created as a prayer, with meditation and fasting being part of the process. They produce beautiful icons at very reasonable prices.

It was at Holt that I met Jean Vanier, who founded the L'Arche communities for disabled people. We were both having a lunch prepared by the nuns, but eaten in a different room from them. Their way of life seems less changed by Vatican II than that of the male orders. They appear to have carried out similar changes but in less drastic ways.

Sister Rachel of the Quidenham Nuns commissioned me to take down the very limiting screen that separated them from their visitors but to replace it with a less obtrusive barrier. I also provided guest accommodation for them just outside the convent. They wanted more contact with the church outside their convent but they did not want that contact to affect their way of life.

It was at Quidenham that the famous Sister Wendy Beckett was to be found. She lived on her own in a caravan, within the convent grounds but outside the enclosure. I have seen her come into the convent to fetch food and carry it back to the caravan. She was not introduced and I did not have a chance to talk to her. I wondered whether she shared the sisters' prayer life or prayed on her own. Did she pray in the convent church or in the caravan? Alas! I never found the courage to ask.

One of the most difficult tasks I have undertaken resulted from a call from the charismatic Mother Xavier McMonagle, Mother General of the Tyburn Nuns. She combined the energy and drive of her Australian heritage with the quality of monastic life which enabled her to expand her congregation in their original convents. She also founded new convents in several countries. She was very impressive, and a blessing to work with. She wanted me to solve the problem of dampness in the basement of their convent, since the architects they were using had been unsuccessful. One of our partners, John Newton, had been commissioned to build the church for the convent prior to World War II so it was rather special to be involved again with this important catholic shrine.

We discovered the dampness was due to oil leaks from storage tanks in an adjoining property. The oil was breaking down the damp proof course in the basement walls of the convent. We were next asked to replace the repaired war-damaged front of part of the convent and to carry out miscellaneous internal works. The practice still acts for the convent but my own personal involvement is now limited to membership of the congregation. They have an annual lecture on catholic issues given by a celebrity. I have found these interesting, and those by Cherie Blair, Chris Patten and Giles Brandreth particularly memorable. I also act as MC for their annual ecumenical service commemorating the visit of Pope John Paul II to Canterbury and I hope to continue to do so for as long as I can still get into my cassock. It had, apparently, belonged to Abbot Rossiter. I have forgotten how I came by it – the only clue is that we are the same height!

CHAPTER 29

Conventions

London 1974

My most exciting convention will always be the one I organised in London in 1974. It was the first Serra International Convention to be held outside the American continent. The chief executive of Serra at that time was Harry O'Haire. He was correct in thinking that we would have difficulty in finding facilities capable of holding the 1,000 people we expected, but then he also believed that we would fail to attract that number of delegates. In fact, we exceeded this number, though we were never sure of the exact figure since most of the Serrans brought wives and many children, and although we had special programmes laid on for them many chose to do their own thing and did not register with the convention. However, when they saw something on the programme that appealed to them they attended without registering or paying! The number registered was 1,016 but 1,036 sat down for the final banquet and the Guildhall stewards claimed that they had mechanically counted 1,129 for the 'Old English Buffet' we held there.

Harry was right about the difficulties we would face, but solving them was an interesting exercise. No hotel was able, in 1974, to take everyone, so we gave people a choice of accommodation, and a pre-booking room price in hotels on Park Lane and Bayswater Road. This made it easy for coaches picking up and dropping off to do so without our having to force people to get into the particular coach we had allocated to their hotel. All coaches were able to go to all hotels. The Serrans staying in the Bayswater Road could reach the events in the HQ Hotel (The Grosvenor House, Park Lane) by walking through Hyde Park.

The Grosvenor House Hotel was chosen as the HQ for the conference because it was the only hotel at that time that could handle the catering. It was a happy coincidence that I knew the general manager, George Lehrian. He was a great help and provided me with a lovely suite free of charge.

I wanted to follow the tradition of providing a no cost hospitality event, of the sort sponsored by most foreign convention cities, but those responsible for London tourism were not prepared to do it. They were confident that such incentives would not increase the number of visitors to London, so we had to make our own arrangements. As our budget was already stretched I made a deal with a coach company to send coaches to the Grosvenor House Hotel at ten minute intervals until there was nobody left. These took people on a pub crawl for a cost of £5, collected by the driver. Fortunately, the drivers chose different pubs; and everyone had a merry evening tour of London at no cost to us.

Our opening mass was celebrated in Westminster Cathedral by Cardinal John Heenan who, in his address, gave his long held view that the Americans should never have called our organisation after Friar Junipero Serra because nobody outside America had heard of him, and that St Thomas More would have been more appropriate because he was already a saint and everybody had heard of him. People still remember this part of his homily and enjoy reminding me of it.

Our twenty guest bishops were invited by the Cardinal to join him for lunch, at which he sought to make the point that the standard of living he had experienced in the States was not to be found in London. He served them a one course casserole dish on their laps, followed by coffee.

I had, unfortunately, failed to persuade the Cardinal to be our guest of honour at the final banquet. He felt that sitting between two people for an entire evening was not a proper use of his time. He also did not like our choice of venue and remained unconvinced by my explanation that the Grosvenor House was the only place in London able to feed 1,000 people in one sitting. I had, however, got to know Cardinal Cordeiro of Karachi, a guest of the convention, who was staying with Cardinal Heenan. I had offered him the use of my suite for a rest in the afternoon, which gave me the opportunity to mention to him the problems with our Cardinal and he kindly offered to tackle him at breakfast the following morning. He was partially successful for Cardinal Heenan did agree to receive everyone before the banquet.

The presentations and the workshops were all well received, the highlights being the opening presentation by Cardinal John Wright, a great humourist from the States who exceeded his allotted time: he said he felt safe in a diocese whose cathedral was not only not finished on time but was still not finished. The talk by Gerard Humphries, a barrister from the North Cheshire Serra (later to become a circuit judge), was the first given by a layman at our conventions and received a standing ovation. Another precedent was the ordination of two Serrans to the diaconate as part of a mass in the ballroom. They were Nigel Bourne, a past president of the London Serra who had made a name for himself as the supervising director of the M1, the first UK motorway, and Joseph Gannon, a Serran from Minneapolis who was famous for being the man who invented the machine for putting holes in donuts.

The really spectacular events were the social ones: the Past Presidents' dinner at Woburn, and the District Governors' dinner in Painters' Hall. This was probably the first time that any of us had experienced the loving cup ceremony, where a ceremonial cup with a cover is passed from standing diner to standing diner, one holding the cover while the other drinks. The custom is said to have originated in the precaution of keeping the right, or 'dagger' hand, employed so that the person who drinks may be assured of no treachery.

Everyone was invited to a buffet supper at The Guildhall where the International President, Albert Maggio, and his board received the hierarchy, catholic members of Parliament, representatives from the American Embassy, leading catholic laymen and the Serrans and their families. The host Serrans wore white tie and tails, and acted as ushers to assist at the Old English Buffet – a very attractive spread of meats, cheeses and pies, together with boars' heads with apples in their mouths. The coaches taking people to The Guildhall were making several journeys and I was not aware that this was happening because it had caused no trouble. When it came to going home at the end of the evening, however, it emerged that different coaches were involved and the drivers had not been told that more than one journey would be needed. Before I realised this was the case the staff of The Guildhall had, not unreasonably, asked the rest of us to leave. Some 600 people, therefore, were left on the pavement until I became aware of the problem and was able to order more coaches. I managed to get them to sing all the old pub songs they had learnt on the pub crawls so, rather than getting upset, everyone was happy to wait for their transport, even though it took over an hour for it to arrive.

The convention ended with a banquet in the HQ Hotel. I had planned to sit on the top table, which for the first time in Serra was designed to take the wives as well as the Board and their guests. However, all the wives, including those who had not registered, took seats at the table, which meant there were insufficient places. The only way this could be resolved was to ask the English Serrans entitled to sit there to find places elsewhere, which they obligingly did. I now felt free to wander around the room and talk to the many people I had met that week. As I passed one of the entrances I became aware of the Welsh Guards tuning their instruments. Tracing the sound to where they were changing into their dress uniform, I was able to ask them not to play, in order to keep this attraction a surprise until after the meal. It was a great success. The Americans were especially appreciative.

Genoa 1995

When I heard that the International Convention was to be held in Genoa I thought it would be good to improve on the idea I had had in 1983, when we hired a coach to take the British contingent to Rome. It had been particularly successful in attracting my fellow Serrans to attend. As a result sixteen more people had come to the Rome convention than had attended the most popular convention venue, New Orleans.

I planned a route which involved taking the Portsmouth-Caen night ferry and driving via Ars, the home of the patron saint of priests, on a three day drive to Genoa. There were already included in the convention programme optional trips to Rome for an audience with the Holy Father, and to Florence for sightseeing. Our return journey would last a week and include visits to Bologna, Padua, Verona, Innsbruck, Oberammergau, Stuttgart, Rüdesheim, Liège, Bruges, and Ostende where we would embark on the ferry for Dover.

In an attempt to minimise the disadvantage of travelling for long periods of time with conversation limited to one's immediate neighbours, I decided to hire a seventy seat double-decker coach, the lower deck of which was quite spacious, having only sixteen seats, eight of which were arranged around tables. It also contained a little kitchen and toilet. It acted as an encouragement to people upstairs to come downstairs to stretch their legs.

In an attempt to justify the seventy seats I wrote to all the English speaking Serrans I had got to know from my twenty-five previous visits to Serra international conventions. I described our proposed trip and said we were aiming for it to be as international as possible. I offered to organise their accommodation in London, before and after the trip, at the Grosvenor Hotel, where we would stop to collect them and drop them off. In the end, seventy-six people booked: thirty-five English, six Scots, twenty-four Americans, six Canadians, and five Australians.

I sent a questionaire to everyone on the tour to be returned a month before we left, together with a passport photograph. This enabled me to give each passenger a booklet containing the names of the driver and my organising team, our itinerary, a biography of the participants and an analysis of those biographies. Each one page biography had a copy of the traveller's photograph, name, position held in Serra, occupation, church and community memberships, sports, interests, children (with a little about what they were doing at school or work). The analysis of the biographies showed who represented the different countries, what professions they might share, who were in similar organisations, what the children had in common. Some of the answers were excellent but others were incomplete so I had to do some editing and the book had the following foreword:

> *The content of these biographies is based on your answers to specific questions, but they have been translated, edited and amplified by your tour leader in the earnest hope that they will stimulate new friendships between Serrans and their families from different continents, through conversation, and without causing the kind of offence that cannot, in true friendship, be rectified. If you are reading this foreword then the effort put into compiling this book will have been justified.*

The booklet also contained three different seating plans for alternate days; within these plans people allocated to the lower deck were given the chance of sitting at a table with the additional facility of being able to play a selection of games if they wished. These booklets were a great success.

All my team were resident on the lower deck, which gave people another reason for coming down, either for business with the treasurer, Michael Bolger, or just for information. Peter and Joan Wurr would serve coffee after we set off first thing in the morning. Just before midday, and again mid-afternoon, they served gin & tonic or soft drinks. We had thought we could be more ambitious with the choice of drinks, but we had underestimated the time it takes to serve seventy people in a coach. Merely obtaining and loading the ingredients for such a number was frightening, especially as they all expected ice with their drinks.

When we stopped to pick up our overseas Serrans at the Grosvenor on the first morning, Ed Reynolds, an American District Judge, produced some eighty dark pink fluorescent caps with 'Serra' printed on them. The immediate reaction was not to wear them. However, a few Americans put them on and by the end of the day it became obvious that they were invaluable. When trying to get everyone back on board after one of our stops they helped differentiate us from other people. In crowded situations we could see all our members from quite long distances. During one lunch break we lost our only teenager, Sean McCloskey, who had wandered off from his parents, each of whom thought he was with the other. We could not see him anywhere but when we reported his loss to the police they put out a call and his hat was spotted within minutes.

The ferry crossings were calm and our overseas visitors enjoyed their cabins. Very few people from the States would have had the opportunity of travelling by boat. It was a pleasant novelty for them. They were well rested for the 415 mile drive to Ars, but were tired by the time we reached the hotel. The hotel was an attractive old coaching inn built around a courtyard, and I had chosen it because we had stayed there before on the Rome trip and I knew it to be good. But when I went to reception I was told that we had arrived late and they had given most of our rooms to a German group. They could accommodate some of us in the main hotel, but the remainder would have to stay in a modern annex a few streets away. I was very angry and told them that I would take our group to the next town. When I got back to the coach and explained what had happened, however, there was unanimous objection to going anywhere else. Everyone was tired so I had to go back and accept what was available. The next morning I was sitting in the guide's seat at the front of the coach when the driver, Glyn Cheeseman, expressed surprise at the route I had chosen going *through* the Alps rather than *over* them. He explained that having to put up with the exhaust fumes produced by lorries in the tunnels was dreadful and he avoided it whenever he could. I asked him if he had ever driven a coach over the Alps, and he replied that he did so every winter when he was taking parties to the ski resorts. I was sure that our Serrans would love to go over the top, so he managed to take the coach that way and the views in the sunshine were spectacular.

When we reached the national boundary post the officials came out and waved us to stop. They congratulated us on being the first double-decker coach they had seen making the attempt over the pass. I asked Glyn what exactly he drove when taking the skiers and he admitted that it was a somewhat shorter and single wheelbase vehicle especially designed for the Alps. He had not realised that this coach might be more difficult.

Almost as soon as we commenced the descent on the Italian side the hairpin bends became much tighter than we had experienced on the way up. Glyn was only just negotiating them by backing up and then going forward several times, which made some of the passengers at the front of the upper deck feel ill. Their fears were exacerbated by the design of the coach, the front of which was some six feet past the front wheels so that as the coach went round a bend one got the impression one was about to plummet over the edge. We had to let some of them stand on the lower deck. The morning and midday prayers we said with our chaplains, Monsignor Jim Kidder and Fathers Frank Hegarty, Anthony Cogliolo and Larry McGovern were never more necessary.

After we had travelled some distance and were backing up on the tightest hairpin we had yet encountered the back of the coach sank into the tarmac and would go no further. Glyn drove the few inches forward that were available, but this was not sufficient to make the turn. We were stuck. We got out and wondered what to do next. We were soon joined by the occupants of the cars behind who could not pass us. They were beginning to form quite a queue. Someone fetched blocks of wood, kept for this purpose on the difficult corners, and told us to put them behind the back wheels and reverse over them, but the wheels had sunk too deeply into the tarmac. We were on the brink of despair when we were joined by a man of authority whose occupation was helping drivers out of trouble on these roads during the winter. We were fortunate to catch him as he was just leaving the area for his holidays. He told us that the blocks of wood had first to be put in front of the wheels, then Glyn was to drive forward. We pointed out that the coach was already too close to the metal rail, but he told us the coach would bend the rail and our driver had only to drive two feet forward over the edge to be able to reverse over the blocks. Glyn was very frightened but he did what he was told. It worked and we were soon getting everybody back onto the coach.

As we were boarding, an Italian policeman arrived on a motorbike to see what was happening. When he saw the damaged tarmac he told Glyn he must report to the police station at the bottom of the mountain to give them his details. This would enable them to extract the cost of the repairs from his company. When the policeman had left, Glyn declared that he had no intention of giving them the details they wanted – but as it happened he had no choice. When we eventually reached the village without further difficulty the same policeman was waiting in the road outside the police station.

The rest of our journey to Genoa was uneventful. Genoa is a coastal town with a railway that attempts to follow a very indented coastline. This is achieved by bridges which enable the railway to cross over the roads in a number of places. The clear headroom of these bridges, however, was less than was needed for our coach. We therefore had to travel greater distances to reach the many venues: the Sheraton Hotel where we were staying, the convention centre, the basilica of Santa Maria Assunta, the Cathedral of St Lawrence, the International Fair building for the banquet, the Ducal Palace for the mayoral reception, the Villa Grimaldi for the theme night of folk music, dance and Genovese cuisine, the Carlo Felice Opera House to hear I Pagliacci and Il Tabarro and the Manuelina Villa for the Past International Presidents' dinner, of which there were eight in the party. We were, however, able to use the coach for all our travel. We did not have to walk or spend time finding taxis. The coach also attracted friends wanting to travel between venues with us, even though we were able to offer them only standing room. Maybe it was our gin & tonic service that was the attraction. I had expected providing the facilities needed for large numbers in Genoa would be as difficult as in London. As it turned out it was clear the organisers had had even greater difficulty, especially when it came to feeding everyone.

By the time we had reached Verona on our way home I had learnt how difficult it was to lead a tour of some seventy people. The knowledge availed me little, however, for when I went to the reception desk to book a tired group in at about eight in the evening I was told the chef had already had a very busy evening and was not prepared to cook for another group. The hotel was on the outskirts of town and getting everyone into town to look for restaurants or even collect 'takeaways' was out of the question. I approached George Lehrian, the general manager of the Grosvenor House in London, a guest of one of our Serrans, in the hope that he might know the Italian group manager. He knew him well and said I might use the manager's name in my negotiations. When I found the manager of our hotel, he was already aware of the problems with our meal and apologised. I explained that a friend of mine in the group knew the group manager very well. He said that made the situation easier, and was quite sure the chef would be pleased to prepare a meal for friends of the group manager's friends. We dined remarkably well on very good steak, followed by an excellent dessert.

In Oberamergau we went to the theatre to see the exhibition of costumes, sets and photographs of the Passion Play. Many of us had seen the play and this made the exhibition much more interesting. After the theatre we went to the famous Bier Keller and as it was a warm day we attempted to drink two-litre steins of good German beer. The most difficult part of the exercise is to hold the stein, for when full it is very much heavier than it looks.

In Rudesheim we stayed in the Hotel Traube Aumüller. I had good reason to remember it for we had stayed there on our way back from the Rome convention. We had ended a very tiring day with a drink to celebrate the golden anniversary of the Maloneys, then turned in early. The following morning Donal Maloney came down for breakfast looking very much hungover. He said it was very kind of us to have arranged for the refrigerator with the great choice of alcohol to be sent to their room as a present. "We should not have drunk it all but once we got started it seemed to be the right thing to do. Philomena does not feel like breakfast and is doing the packing." We told him we were not responsible for the refrigerator, that it was now customary for most hotels to provide one in the rooms and that one was supposed to pay for what one had used on leaving the hotel. He did not believe us and apparently left without paying for his mini-bar. It couldn't happen nowadays.

I am sure that the hotel did not recognise us from the last visit, but they were about to have reason for remembering this stay. I had come down from my room ready for the evening and was chatting to other members of the party near the reception desk in the lounge hall when Kath Treloar hurried to the reception desk to ask for an ambulance. Les was very ill. She thought that he had suffered a stroke. The ambulance arrived quickly, bringing a doctor and heart revival equipment which they carried up to the bedroom. At first the news was hopeful but, shortly afterwards, Les died. Those of us who had not already started praying did so now. His death had a devastating effect on the party. A cheerful Australian architect who specialised in building the facilities at race tracks, he had effortlessly made friends with everybody and had become an important part of our group. Now, without any warning, he was dead.

That night we had arranged to have a wild boar and beer evening in the famous Rüdesheimer Schloss. In the circumstances, many thought it seemed wrong to have that kind of entertainment. But we had made reservations so we went ahead. In the excitement of the Schloss we forgot Les and Kath, and I am ashamed to say that we had a good evening.

The following day was our last before the drive for home. We arrived in Bruges just in time to take the last canal boat. It took us via the canals through a large part of my favourite European city before we booked into our hotel for the night. After we had changed we met for our usual hospitality drinks before dinner. Everyone was very generous with their praise, telling me it had been a marvellous holiday. We had certainly achieved a great deal in two weeks. It was as well, however, that we celebrated before we reached London, for when we got to Victoria we had great difficulty in persuading a policeman to let us stop, even to unload the luggage of the overseas Serrans outside the Scandic Crown Hotel. He was certainly not going to let us chat on the pavement.

CHAPTER 30

The Pubs

I was first attracted to the Highgate pubs when we had the office in Fairbridge Road. I would mark the end of the working week by taking our staff on the 271 bus to the village on a Friday evening. Over the years we used several different pubs for very different reasons. We were attracted by the large prawns tucked over an even larger brandy glass full of mayonnaise which stood on the counter of The Red Lion & Sun. We liked to sit on a summer's evening outside The Flask in the square, the only pub where this was possible in those days; the snacks were good there too. Another favourite was The Prince of Wales because it was nearest to the bus stop and had a very friendly landlord. It was also the haunt of another architect who had his office in the village.

When the office moved into the village, we occasionally had lunch in The Angel which served excellent food. 'The Goons' (Peter Sellers, Spike Milligan and Harry Secombe) were often to be found there, taking a break from their script writing sessions. They never stopped larking about. On one occasion, impatient with the slow service from the kitchen, they launched a protest by lying outstretched on their backs on the floor, preventing any other customers from coming in.

I liked to have an occasional after work drink in the nearest pub to the new office, The Duke's Head. I don't remember the couple who owned it when I started going there, but it was soon taken over by John Murphy who, though he had no history of working in the trade, was committed to creating an interesting environment in one of the least interesting pubs in the area. He attracted some interesting people too. As I got to know them I went there more often. The first to arrive would be Ian Downing, scientific advisor to the cabinet. He could be found doing *The Times* crossword puzzle from 5.30 pm most days. He was a Methodist and we enjoyed discussing religion. Not long afterwards, Mike Warner would arrive. Mike was the Canadian owner of 'Chief in the Box' and an astute business man. Bob Spearman, the artist, came in quite early and Peter Clarkson, the cancer surgeon, would also be early if he was coming. For several months during the best years, Chris Mann and John Devaney graced us with their presence. They had recently won the TV Journalists of the Year award for their coverage of 'Time Share'. An interesting addition to the party was a young man in the KGB. He had a son at Highgate School and never went back to the Soviet Union when they closed down the Russian Sugar Corporation, his 'cover' at that time. He still lives in Highgate. His father, a high ranking officer in the KGB, came to the pub a few times while he was on holiday in the UK. In the background, and making only the occasional contribution to our discussions, was the strange lady from MI5 Russian Section and her minder. The minder had a great singing voice and was certainly the more vocal of the two. She too is still to be seen in Highgate. Another occasional visitor was a Major-General who lived on the other side of the road, next to the optician. None of these seemed especially guarded in their conversation together – unless, perhaps, they were speaking in code!

Several of these acquaintances developed into long-term friends. Chris Mann and Stephanie invited me to their wedding in Hillsborough, Northern Ireland. Stephanie's parents and relatives lived there, and although Hillsborough was not their home it was felt to be the safest place in what was a dangerous country at that time. Hillsborough Castle, of course, is the residence of the Secretary of State for Northern Ireland.

The town was very protestant and they asked me not to embarrass anyone by enquiring where the Catholic church was because there is no Catholic church in the town or anywhere near it. On the Sunday morning I awoke early, had breakfast in the hotel and went for a walk in the park. When I arrived at a church on the edge of the park I suddenly realised it was Pentecost Sunday and decided to go in to say a few prayers. However, this was not as easy as I had expected. All the seats were box pews with doors which seemed to be locked. I was later told that the Queen used this church for worship when she stayed at her official residence of Hillsborough Castle. Her Majesty would process down the wider than normal main aisle and the doors would be locked. But I did manage to open one of the doors and, as I prayed, I became even more concerned that I would be missing mass on this Holy Day of Obligation. I checked the times of the services in the porch and found that there was one at eleven o'clock. It was then a little after 10.00 am so I decided to return for the service. When I did so I found a considerable number of people in the narthex. I introduced myself to one of them and asked if I could sit anywhere. Before he could answer a voice reminiscent of Ian Paisley's boomed at me: "Are you a visitor. I would like to welcome you. I am the vicar." He led me into the church and walked me down the aisle to the front. Then, on second thoughts, he led me to a seat at the back of the church.

It was a very impressive liturgy. The homily was directed to the youngsters, who had been gathered around the vicar in the centre of the church. He illustrated his Pentecost theme with a full size skeleton. The children were enthralled, and so was I. At the end of the liturgy he baptised two babies in the font at the back of the church, close to where I was sitting. It was then I realised why he had changed his mind about where I should sit. He really was very thoughtful. The other advantage of my position was that I was able to by-pass the baptismal families and be among the first out of church. The vicar, however, was there before me. He asked what I thought of the service. I was complimentary and he asked whether I was a regular church goer in England. I said I was. He asked me the name of my parish, and I realised I was in trouble. When I answered, "St Josephs", he responded, "Ah. You are a papist." I agreed. He thought for a second, then said, "I am not against papists." After another pause, he added, "But then we don't have any papists in Hillsborough."

The only one of the many pub friends whom I still see regularly is Mike. He has sold 'Chief in the Box' and is now in the process of selling the offices he received instead of money from the sale, part of a compulsory purchase arrangement to make way for the new Arsenal Emirates Stadium.

Because The Duke's Head is no longer the pub of choice, we spend most Friday evenings in The Angel for a short, two pint session, talking about holidays, property and how Mike can make millions buying and selling on the stock market. The Angel is a rather basic pub which tends to attract a young 'after work' crowd together with a number of older men who enjoy their company. If the weather is good we might walk a little further to sit outside The Flask, but we do this less often now that the landlord has partially covered the outside seating area with a roof. The Flask is where I met my wife, Fiona – but that is a story told elsewhere in this book.

CHAPTER 31

The NHS

In 1976 I was appointed by Haringey Council to be a generalist member on the Haringey health authority where I remained for some fifteen years, the last four as vice-chairman to Laurie Bains. The chief executive was Barbara Young, who left us to be chief executive of the new St Mary's Hospital, Paddington, and subsequently became a member of the House of Lords.

The Board was made up of executive directors, members chosen by medical and non-medical staff, and generalist members appointed by the local council. Nobody was paid for this work. We met in the lecture room at St Ann's academic building, chosen because it was large enough to accommodate several rows of chairs for the public. There were always members of the public in attendance at our meetings in those days.

The NHS was still evolving and there were many changes and closures to existing buildings. The meetings were highly political in tone, largely because political appointees made up fifty per cent of the board. These were mostly serving councillors on Haringey Council and the battles between the parties in the council were continued in the Authority. I tended to lead for the Conservatives, while Bernie Grant, one of our first black Members of Parliament, led for Labour. The debates on several occasions were encouraged by the large number of protesters who crowded into the back of the room, the majority of these being mothers with their pre-school children who had little respect for what the meeting was trying to achieve. Some of our members were nervous so, being the tallest and most aggressive looking man, I was seated close to the public to discourage them from attempting to enter the members' area.

I was also a mental health manager. This made me responsible for people who were 'sectioned' and deprived of their normal rights. In effect I was expected to visit them in the wards to check on their care and to be one of three managers hearing appeals against, or renewals of, the section. At this time we were called to adjudicate very rarely. Patients were not encouraged to appeal against their section and solicitors were not made as readily available as they are today. Therefore, only three managers were required to look after all the Haringey patients under section.

Our health authority was replaced in 1993 by the New River Health Authority, on which there were no political appointees. We were interviewed and, if found suitable, appointed by the NHS Appointments Commission. We also received a salary. I was asked if I was prepared to become chairman but had to declare that although I could find the time necessary to be an effective member I did not feel I had the time to be an effective chairman. I did, however, feel that I could be vice-chairman and I accepted that position.

This was a different kind of authority, and the meetings were totally different. We were able to concentrate on what was best for the community and although there were differences of opinion they were not based on political dogma. I felt that I was really making a contribution and that the appointment was not taking up more time than I could easily afford. After a while, the Conservative controlled Ministry of Health set up Primary Care Groups. These were groups of practices with their own budget and facility to purchase health from the hospitals for their patients. I was made chairman of the largest of these groups. It was a chance to see the provision of health at grass roots level, which was very satisfying for both the doctors and me. I was sorry when the government changed and the concept was abandoned, but pleased to see that the new administration under David Cameron intends to bring back a version of the same idea. At its simplest it gives the GP the money to purchase what he recommends. The main challenge with the system is to motivate a significant number of GPs, many of whom would prefer not to become involved.

I remained a mental health manager but was appointed to a separate mental health trust where a dozen managers were appointed to deal with the increased workload resulting from the policy of explaining clearly to patients that they were entitled to appeal against being sectioned and the renewal of the section. We received training in understanding mental illness, its treatment and the complexities of the law.

The newly elected government decided to enlarge the authority and we became Enfield and Haringey health authority. I was once again interviewed by the NHS Appointments Commission, and made joint vice-chairman by Peter Nixon, our chairman. He was charming and easy to work with. He was also very effective; we were sorry to lose him to the new University College Hospital. During this phase the budget formerly given to General Practice was now allocated to substantial areas of the Authority and I became a member of the Tottenham Primary Care Group. This proved ineffective, however, and no one was surprised when in 2001 the system was changed.

The Primary Care Trust was created. I was interviewed and

appointed to the Haringey Primary Care Trust as a director by the NHS Appointments Commission. All our directors were new to Haringey and I was seen as something of a father figure. The chairman, Richard Sumray, did not believe in appointing vice-chairmen, but I was asked to take over on the very few occasions he was unable to be present. This was the most effective board I had served on and we made great improvements to the system.

A further change was that made to local authority district boundaries. Although London was not affected by this it was decided to advertise the posts and reappoint the boards of directors. Our chairman was interviewed by the Appointments Commission and reappointed. Those shortlisted from the advertisement, together with existing directors wishing to remain, were to be interviewed locally by a panel of three: Richard Sumray, another chairman, and a representative of the Appointments Commission. At my assessment review the previous June Richard had commented:

> Gerald continues to make an important contribution to the Board. He asks difficult questions and in so doing ensures that the executive directors are properly held to account. His long experience as a non-executive director in Health is extremely helpful in cutting through some of the minutiae and consequently being able to concentrate on the key issues. He has been very helpful and supportive in the recent period when our budget has had to be adjusted downwards. He has also been a strong support to our new chair of audit whom he has guided well and appropriately. He remains an invaluable board member.

I therefore went into my interview confident that, although I would be eighty before a normal four year contract came to an end, I was still fit and could provide evidence of my ability to fill the post.

One aspect of the interview concerned me, however. I was not asked any appropriate questions by the interviewer from the Appointments Commission. She asked only one question, which was about one of my honours. That indicated to me that I was either very 'in' or very 'out'.

When I was told by Richard that I was not to be reappointed, his only comment was: "I am sorry, but you did not interview well." To make the situation worse they failed to appoint the number of directors required, ending up two short and having to re-advertise. My initial reaction was not to blame them or do anything about it, but I was irritated that an agency of the government should choose to ride roughshod over government policy. I also believe that older people in good health do not become less effective as they grow older; only when their health fails should they be required to resign.

When later I was asked by our Human Resources Executive Director if I was satisfied about the fairness of the decision, I felt I had to say no. He said he would come back to me. When he did, he told me that as I was employed by the NHS Appointments Commission, not the NHS, it was not his responsibility. Needless to say, I was never asked by the NHS Appointments Commission for my opinion.

Nevertheless, I am still an associate director and mental health manager of the local mental health trust. I am also a governor of the Whittington Hospital.

Just prior to ceasing to be a director of the Primary Care Trust I was head hunted by the London Deanery to be a lay chairman for the London Deanery recruitment programme. They have a specialist training programme for consultant grade doctors. Junior grade doctors have to apply to prove themselves suitable for this training. I have become a lay assessor of this training programme. This fills the gap left by the Primary Care Trust – and there is no age limit.

CHAPTER 32

The Judiciary

I have been very fortunate in winning the few cases I have had to answer in court. Early in the life of the practice I went to court to claim fees for obtaining a planning consent. I had accepted a commission to enlarge an existing drivers' snack bar on an A road. Our client was anxious to improve the value of his site in the unlikely event that the A road would become one of the new motorways, whereupon he hoped his site would then be required for the creation of a service station, much more valuable use for the land. The intention to build the motorway was announced prior to our getting the consent and it may be that the announcement influenced the planning committee to decide in our favour. It has to be admitted that our fees were a little on the high side but that was because we felt we were entitled to benefit from the increase in value. The client did not agree and refused to pay us anything. The judge, however, found in our favour, gave us full costs, and increased the fee still further to compensate us for the delay in obtaining our fees and for the time we had spent briefing our legal advisors.

I have already told you about our case before the Hampstead Magistrates when the local council, at the behest of some of our neighbours, charged us with making too much noise. The local police gave evidence on our behalf and the magistrates ruled in our favour.

There was, however, a case I lost which I feel I should not have lost. I was charged with parking on a zebra crossing. When I went to court and the charge was read out, the zebra crossing on which it was claimed I had parked was not the one on which I had actually been parked. The two crossings were at either end of Highgate village and the charge had been made out for the wrong crossing. I pleaded 'not guilty' on the grounds that I had not parked on the zebra crossing in the charge. This was a valid plea. The Chairwoman asked me if I had parked on another crossing and I admitted that I had, although not on the one in the charge sheet. She said: "You were on a zebra crossing. You broke the law. Pay a fine of £50." When I stood down from being a councillor in Haringey I was asked by Miss Curtis, one of our head teachers, if I would become a magistrate. I agreed, and found my interview panel was being chaired by the same chairwoman before whom I had appeared. I now know her to be Betty Killip. When I was accepted and sworn in at Southwark Crown Court she was my sponsor as she was the chairwoman of the Highgate Bench, to which I was assigned. The zebra crossing incident was never mentioned and we worked well together. I often wonder whether she realised I had appeared before her and received a fine.

There are few other situations where three people have to agree on a decision as often and in such a short period of time as on a bench of magistrates – sometimes as often as forty times in half a day. Magistrates come from diverse walks of life, follow different political and religious beliefs and are of varying ages. One learns a great deal about different walks of life on the bench and I developed considerable respect for the more experienced magistrates.

One is often asked what sentencing people is like. It is difficult to give an answer without sounding like someone in

Social Services. Only a few of the people who appear in court have not appeared there before, or will not be appearing there again after they have served their sentence. Very few of them work for a living; some have never worked. Virtually none is part of a stable family. The only sign of hope is that the figures indicate that the number of their appearances decreases as they get older. In modern parlance, "We don't do pensioners." The exceptions provide us with opportunities to be constructive.

I was chairing in No.1 Court one morning when I noticed, sitting at the back in their kippahs and tallits, two orthodox Jewish lads, one about thirteen, the other about eighteen years of age. I thought they were probably there for educational purposes but as time passed I decided to ask the clerk. He told me that the young one had spent the night in the cells after being arrested for being drunk and disorderly. The older one, his uncle, was there because he was under age. The lad had pleaded with the jailer to call his young uncle rather than his parents. Traditionally, drunks are placed last on the morning list to give them time to dry out. I decided, however, that the Jewish boy had already suffered enough and called his case on next. The uncle gave his evidence very well. Apparently, the nephew had been to a bar mitzvah, tried some of the drink and, deciding he liked it, drank more and more. He did not know it was alcoholic. Eventually, realising he was drunk, he left the celebration to avoid being discovered in an inebriated condition. He had attempted to walk home down the middle of the road and the police had arrested him. His uncle also explained what a criminal record would do for a young person in their culture. Happily, I managed to persuade my bench to find him not guilty.

On another occasion a very distressed lady was shown into court and taken to the witness box. She was handed a bible and told to swear that she was who she said she was, namely the mother of a soldier killed in action. She was obliged to appear in court and go through this process in order to receive medal for bravery posthumously. Del ".

Other exceptions occur in the area of fraud or deceit. Crimes of this nature are not normally committed by the deprived but by the more affluent and respectable members of society.

A man who had come to England from the colonies was brought before the court by the local authority to recover the local tax he had failed to pay: some £40,000. He pleaded that he was without the means to pay. An investigation into his affairs, however, showed that he was employing ten men to collect the rents from flats he had created from single houses. He had managed to buy these houses for his family with loans raised from different local authorities. His case had come to court only because an unexpected rise in the interest rates on what he owed meant that the cost of servicing these loans exceeded the rent his employees were collecting for him.

Contrary to what I have been given to understand by other members of the judiciary, the courts have not provided me with amusing incidents. The only one I can think of occurred in the following case.

A man was charged with larceny and pleaded 'not guilty'. After the prosecution had presented its case, the defendant was brought into the witness box. Now that I was looking directly at him I realised I knew him. I had never spoken to him but he had worked for Haringey Council. I interrupted the proceedings to declare that I knew him but that because my knowledge was not sufficient to influence me I was prepared to continue. I then explained that he was entitled to ask for a retrial. He said he had realised that we knew each other before I had, and had decided that the devil he knew would be better than one he did not! We continued, so neither of us will know whether he was right.

One of the aspects of our training was to gain some knowledge of the various different types of prison. I managed to visit Pentonville, Holloway, Brixton, Feltham and the Chase Farm and Broadmoor hospitals. One does this as a member of a group so it is almost inevitable that one encounters inmates known to one or other members of the group. I was surprised that such people are usually very pleased to see the magistrate who sentenced them. There seems to be no animosity between the judged and the judge.

I was having a glass of beer with friends in The Prince of Wales in Highgate early one evening when a man approached and, somewhat to my embarrassment, said in a voice loud enough for all to hear: "I know this man. He is a magistrate at Highgate Court, but I do have to say he is fair – not like some of the others up there!"

Although most of our hearings fit into specific categories there are also some cases one will never forget.

I arrived at Wood Green Crown Court to sit with a recorder dealing with appeals from our Magistrates Court or cases where the magistrates did not have sufficient powers to sentence. Instead of having to wait to join the recorder at ten o'clock I was taken by his clerk straight to his room. He explained we had a problem and he wished to share it with me. He had almost no experience of being a judge, and his area of expertise as a barrister was divorce. Earlier that morning, he had been approached by defence council to hear a case of appeal against sentence in camera, the reason being that if we upheld the sentence of imprisonment his client's life would be at risk. The recorder had refused to hear the case in chambers. He had then received a similar request from the prosecution and likewise refused it. He was now being asked to see a representative of the Commissioner of Police. He was hoping I would support his decisions and follow the same course of action with the police; I did. We decided to commence the case in open court, but then proceed in camera.

It was relatively straightforward. The defendant, a woman of about thirty, had defrauded Social Security of some £30,000, and she had previous history of a similar charge. The magistrates had sentenced her to six months in prison. Having established this, we asked everyone not directly involved in the case to leave. Then, with the agreement of both councils, we called the police to read the commissioner's letter. It stated that the defendant was prepared to give evidence in a case involving an attack on a policeman in the Broadwater Farm estate, from which he had died, and the police were convinced that if this became known while she was in Holloway her life would be at risk. We did not send her to prison but gave her the opportunity of repaying the amount she had defrauded in instalments. She was certainly very lucky. We never knew whether she gave the evidence she had promised or, if she did so, if it proved of any value.

Magistrates are not informed of what happens when a case is adjourned or settled in a higher court, unless the case is reported in the press. Normally, this does not matter, but there are important cases where one would like to have known the final decision. It is, for example, still possible to challenge a serious charge of murder or rape by pleading 'no case to answer', and this is heard in a magistrates' court. Because such cases can take many hours, or sometimes days to determine, they are normally listed for one magistrate alone. I heard two of these in my time. The more interesting one was also the simpler. A man was accused of raping his girlfriend. They were both Catholics who had met at university and had jointly agreed not to have sexual intercourse before marriage. They received their first degrees and both stayed on at university to take their Master's. In their second year, at the May Ball, they both had a little too much to drink and the evening ended with intercourse. He maintained that she had agreed but she insisted that she had not consented and he had raped her. I did find there was a case to answer and, accordingly, sent it to the Crown Court to be heard. I do not know the outcome, but I would not have wanted to be on the jury in that case.

CHAPTER 33

International President of Serra

I had been on the international board of Serra as a trustee for three years, the first two years representing Europe, then, as we spread throughout Europe, representing Great Britain alone. In my last year I was asked by the nominating committee whether I would be prepared to serve as vice-president with a view to one day becoming president. We were not given an expense allowance in those days and I felt bound to tell them that I did not have the disposable income of previous presidents, so I would not be able spend as much time or money travelling around the world as they had done. I was limited to doing what I could with what I had saved. If they thought that was a sufficient commitment I would be honoured to serve. I said the same thing to the two differently composed nominating committees in the two years that followed, but thereafter I was in a position to state that my savings amounted to some £6,000 and I was prepared to use this sum for Serra. I also committed myself to spending a week in every month for Serra, leaving three weeks for the practice. As a result, I was nominated and duly elected.

In my first month as International President I received an anonymous donation of £1,000 and a surprising number of offers of hospitality. Moreover, my practice seemed to do better without me, and at the end of my year I still had £6,000 in the bank!

I became president in Rio de Janeiro. My inaugural address was given in English during a power failure, which rather upset the interpreters as they were relying on a previously prepared translation. However, after this unfortunate start, my year was effective and enjoyable.

I was aware that as the first non-American president I had a special responsibility for presenting the international character of the organisation. The membership was still largely American; the only convention to be held outside the Americas had been the one in London. Everything about the organisation was American. I took my first international step at my first board meeting, which was held at nine o'clock on the morning after the banquet that had closed the International Convention. I arrived early and placed, together with an agenda, an abbreviated version of English rules of debate in each member's place. I was determined not to use USA rules. I began the meeting as soon as John Donahue, the chief executive, arrived, shortly after 9.00 am. Although not all the members were present when we commenced, everyone had turned up by the time we reached the item: 'Venue for next board meeting'. I proposed we met in Rome, the capital of the Church, as opposed to somewhere close to the international office or in the president's home town. Meeting in Rome would enable us to visit the office of the Congregation for Education and Vocations (the Vatican equivalent of our Ministry of Education) to which Serra is aggregated. Many of the American members objected on the grounds that they had not agreed to serve on a board that held meetings outside the USA. I reminded them that they had agreed to serve on an international board. After further unresolved discussion I called for a secret ballot, as defined in the rules of debate laid on the table before them. They were, not unreasonably, mystified because secret ballots do not exist in the USA. I explained what was meant and John Donahue handed around the pieces of paper with 'Yes' and 'No' printed on them, against which each member would place a cross to indicate his choice. He collected and started to count them. They expected me to declare the result but I said we should move on and deal with it after the next item. When that had been considered I announced that we were going to Rome. The board members wanted to know the votes. I told them that it was against the concept of a secret ballot to reveal these but I would do so on this occasion: nine for, nine against, and I was using my casting vote for the proposal. Someone who had counted the number of voting members present then asked what had happened to the abstentions. In the USA their number is added to the number of those against a proposal. I explained that under English rules the decision was limited to those voting for and against: abstentions were not counted, so we were going to Rome. One or two left at the end of the meeting upset, but the majority accepted the outcome.

After the convention I led some two hundred and fifty Serrans and their wives on a tour of Serra in South America. Because of our number we were never able to travel all together and it frequently took the best part of a day to get everyone into each place on the itinerary. We visited Serra groups in Brazil, Argentina, Paraguay and Peru. These were all new to Serra and having a large group of Serrans visit them from other countries must have been very encouraging for them. It certainly was for us.

When I returned to England I began preparations for the board meeting in Rome. I found it so easy to get an appointment with our Congregation that I tried the others and was delighted when almost all the cardinal prefects of the congregations and councils indicated they were prepared to see us. I was thus able to devise a programme which involved splitting the group into three but added only a day to our meeting. A few minor problems arose because I did not tell the congregations we were trying to see them all, and some were a little unhappy that they did not see the whole group and particularly the president. I also had to pacify some cardinals who were kept waiting while we were tactfully trying to leave their colleagues.

We spent another day seeing St Peter's and having an audience with the holy father in the audience hall. He was able to speak only to the few of us who were in the front row, but I asked him if we could have a photograph of him with the board afterwards and he graciously agreed. There was an attempt by his attendants to stop us leaving the pen but he not only insisted we join him but that our wives should accompany us, so our photographs included the whole party.

Everyone enjoyed the trip, and almost all subsequent boards have visited Rome during their year.

The last duty of the International President is to chair the International Convention at the end of his year of office. In my case it was held in Louisville, Kentucky, at the time of my fiftieth birthday. I arrived at the convention HQ Hotel in advance of the meeting, with my friends, John Evans and John Smith. They were not Serrans but were accompanying me to help with the entertainment and to play some golf. We went to the reception and booked in. Our keys were given to a bell boy who took our luggage to the lift. As we were ascending he asked who was in the owner's penthouse suite and I admitted that it was I. (The international president was always given the best room in the convention hotel, free of charge.) He then looked my casual dress up and down and said: "You must sure be important. The last person to use that suite was Colonel Sanders of the Kentucky Fried Chicken chain." The two Johns were still laughing when we reached the suite.

My accommodation consisted of an entrance hall, which was larger than my living room, giving access to another large room called the library, and a slightly smaller room they termed 'the lounge'. Off the lounge were two palatial bedroom suites with the largest beds I have ever seen, curtained and raised up on a platform two steps off the bedroom floor. I used the lounge for general entertaining and a cocktail party for a hundred guests on my birthday, fifty of whom stayed on for dinner in the library. After the concluding banquet of the convention, the incoming president, Nick Spinella (a great friend) and I gave a joint party in the library and lounge for the best part of two hundred people to mark my departure and his inauguration.

The opening mass of the convention had been in the cathedral and the main concelebrant, Archbishop Thomas McDonough of Louisville. The board and I were in the procession and took the front seats. Just before the final blessing, Father Frank Hegarty, chaplain to London Serra, and one of the concelebrants, approached the archbishop and, after a short conversation, started to read from a piece of parchment:

I, Father Frank Hegarty, have been given the faculty by Cardinal Basil Hume, Archbishop of Westminster, to present Pope John Paul II's award of Knight of Saint Gregory the Great, for his work in promoting and encouraging vocations to the priesthood and religious life, to Gerald Murphy, past International President of Serra.

And I was called forward to receive the medal.

We learnt after the mass that Archbishop McDonough had not been at all happy about the proceeding, since papal awards are normally presented only by bishops, and there were present in the sanctuary more than twelve cardinals, archbishops and bishops who could have presented it. Father Hegarty had been asked to defer to the local bishop but had refused. He thought that a representative of our own cardinal was much more important than a bishop from another land.

I had not been asked whether I would accept the award, so I had the extra pleasure of surprise. My pleasure was tarnished, however, when I found that my mother was not in the cathedral. The people responsible for seeing that she was on the bus had failed to do so, and she had missed the occasion – a bitter disappointment to her and me.

CHAPTER 34

Harvest Festival at
St Peter's

I had decided to spend the day after the Serra International board meeting in Rome relaxing: going to St Peter's for the eleven o'clock mass, having a quiet reflective Italian lunch with a bottle of wine, and getting the plane home in the evening. I said goodbye to the other board members leaving for their various flights. They were being assisted by a Roman Serran who described himself as an 'airline agent'. He had been helpful in organising the physical aspects of our meeting and was certainly able to resolve the odd difficulty that had arisen. He was also adept at improving the routes people planned to use, and he even saved money for a few of them. When he asked me what my plans were, I told him of my intention to go to St Peter's. He said that would be difficult because it would already be full, as it was the Sunday they celebrated the harvest festival and people came from all over Italy. If I was prepared to wait till he had finished what he was doing, however, he would be happy to take me to the basilica and get me a seat.

The hotel was only a fifteen minute walk from St Peter's, but he talked so much to the people leaving that I feared we would not get there in time. Eventually, we crossed the road from the hotel and went through an unobtrusive side door in the wall of Vatican City. My friend, who I now discovered was a Swiss Guard out of uniform, saluted and we walked across a courtyard to an entrance at the back of St Peter's. The door was open; just inside was another Swiss Guard and two gentlemen in morning dress. These, I discovered, are known as gentiluomini. They attend the Pope and manage the events at which he presides. The Swiss Guard saluted and I was introduced to a gentiluomo. He conducted us down a long corridor to the circular area around the altar. It was now obvious that the basilica was very full indeed. At this entrance we encountered another two gentiluomini in morning dress and I was again introduced. One of them was a Serran who would look after me during the mass. He joined us as we crossed beneath the dome to seats I was told were reserved for representatives of the government who were always in attendance at this particular festival. I shook hands with their equivalent to our Prime Minister and then with everyone in the front row. I had hardly recovered from this experience when we approached one of the four sets of sedilia placed an equal distance from each other on the periphery of the circular space. These were already occupied by cardinals, archbishops and bishops in sets of three. My Swiss Guard spoke to the middle of three at one of the sedilia, and one of the bishops on the outside got up and left. I was shown to his seat, only seconds before the choir began the opening hymn announcing the procession of the Holy Father.

It was a truly festive occasion. At the offertory, young men and women in traditional dress, representing each of the Italian regions, processed up the central aisle carrying baskets of their respective region's produce. These were presented to the Holy Father who spoke to each couple while their basket was taken and displayed around the altar.

At the communion about twenty people were marshalled

into a line in the central aisle to receive the sacrament from the Holy Father. When they were assembled the Serran gentiluomo conducted me to this line and placed me at the head of it. I received holy communion from the Holy Father.

I have never managed to discover how this man, my casually dressed Swiss Guard, was able to procure me such a seat at such a prestigious occasion in St Peter's.

CHAPTER 35

Serra around the world

During my year as international president I visited several of the thirty-six countries where Serra existed and I felt a particular responsibility for Spain and Africa because they were still without a national structure or representative on the international board. I visited Spain twice; on the second occasion I chartered Serra in Jerez, a beautiful part of the country where its principle export of sherry gives it great character. The wineries, with their famous names written large on their facades, dwarf the other buildings in the town. Many of these – Harveys, Croft, Harris, Garvey and Booth – remind the visitor of the original involvement of the British. I thought that this historical legacy would have made spoken English fairly commonplace but was surprised to find that my hosts had almost no English. This gave me no alternative but to place myself in their hands and go where they steered me. I merely put the framed charter parchment, mission bell, statue of Friar Junepero Serra and the lapel pins on the altar before mass and waited to react when someone took hold of my arm. Eventually, I was taken up to the altar by an MC who indicated that I should present the charter, bell, and statue, one at a time, to the priest who in turn presented them to the new president. The other members then came forward for their lapel pins. Because I was acting without thinking, and because I had not been party to the planning of the event, I did not realise that there were women in the line to collect their lapel pin in this proudly 'men only' organisation. When the first woman presented her very buxom self I decided there was no way I was going to pin the broach on this lady, so I simply handed it to her and did the same with her colleagues.

After the mass we had a meal to celebrate the charter and it was far too happy an event to try and explain in my very limited Spanish that rules had been broken. I was also probably less shocked than most of my predecessors would have been because in England we had started inviting wives to our meetings, although we refrained from making them members. When I returned home I telephoned John Donahue who explained that in many countries, notably those in South America or Asia, it was impossible to get men to join if their wives were not allowed to go to the meetings, so Serra turned a blind eye to the inevitable. Six years later the delegates at the International Convention decided, by a very small majority, to accept a proposal to open membership to women. Even then it would not have happened had it not been for our recent expansion into the Third World. The majority of the delegates from the USA, Canada, Australia and Scotland voted against the proposal.

My first visit to Africa was to charter a group in Accra, the capital of Ghana. Much of the early work had been started by Frank Metyko, a previous International President from Houston, Texas. His initiative was followed up by Henry Nelson, a committed Catholic and past member of the Kwame Nkrumah government.

Henry picked me up from the airport, and took me to the hotel he had arranged for me. He even inspected my room, assuring me that, despite the cracked hand-basin and the fact that the wardrobe doors were hanging off their hinges, it was probably the best they had to offer. He explained that they did not have many tourists and the hotels were used mostly for parties and similar celebrations.

That evening we had a meeting over our evening meal to design the chartering of their Serra. The Ghanaian Serrans were disappointed to find there would be no elaborate ceremony. Our custom was simply to present the framed charter, a missionary bell and a statue of our patron to the new president, and lapel pins to the members. The bell was normally presented by the sponsoring Serra. In this case, my own London Club had donated the bell and I had it with me. The abundant literature explaining our purpose and how we could promote and encourage vocations would have already been sent to them. It was past midnight before we settled on the final details of the ceremony.

The chartering took place at midday in the cathedral, the archbishop of Accra being the celebrant. The new president and I led the new members in a procession behind the archbishop. The new members were seated in the reserved front rows, and the president and myself on the presbyterium, he on one side of the archbishop and I on the other. The charter, bell, statue and lapel pins were already on the altar. The ceremony began after a homily which stressed the importance of priesthood and the responsibility the laity had for promoting and encouraging vocations to the priesthood and religious life. It ended by recommending membership to a packed congregation that included the leaders of all the Diocesan lay organisations.

After the homily, two altar boys came in procession behind the crucifix, carrying a copy of the wooden throne used to install the King of the Ashanti Tribe and placed it in front of the altar. The MC then called me and the new president to come before the archbishop, who was standing in front of the throne. The Archbishop asked the president to swear to perform all those duties prescribed in the president's manual, from which the archbishop read. When the new president had made his promises the archbishop and I lowered him onto the throne three times: the first in the name of the Father, the second in the name of the Son, and the third in the name of the Holy Spirit. He then remained on the throne and was handed the charter, bell and statue, as each one was blessed at the altar. Finally, I attached the president's lapel pin

The secretary and the treasurer were called forward next and the archbishop read out their duties from their respective manuals. They swore before the archbishop that they would carry out each of the duties he had listed. I then presented them with a lapel pin blessed by the archbishop. After this all the members advanced one by one before the archbishop to swear to undertake their duties and to receive their pins from me. The ceremony ended with enthusiastic clapping which lasted until we had all returned to our seats; then mass continued.

After mass everyone gathered in the adjoining courtyard, where excellent exchanges took place among the Serrans, their guests and the other organisations present, but there was no meal. Henry, his wife, a few of his friends and I went to his home for lunch.

On another visit I went 'up country' to the town of Kumasi where they were trying to start Serra in the university. I stayed for a few days with Bishop Peter Kwasi Sarpong in his residence. It was a simple home built on stilts treated to protect the occupants from unwanted creatures climbing up into the house. It had a large open-plan living area, with bookcases at one end and a circular dining table seating eight people at the other. Off the dining area was a small oratory, no larger than seven feet by five. When we had mass in the morning there was just enough space for the bishop and his secretary to squeeze in behind a small altar, and for me to stand just in front of it. The mass was straightforward, unadorned, and we all prayed for everyone we knew who needed prayers for any reason. Time is never the essence of their liturgies.

At meal times the secretary would come in with people he had found to fill the empty seats at table. Meals consisted of bowls full of local vegetables and three bowls of a mild curried soup each with a small piece of the meat or fish that had flavoured it in the centre. This was used to make the vegetables more palatable. I was invited to take the pieces in the centre of the bowls. I broke a small portion off each and, although I was urged to take more, declined to do so; the remaining pieces were then offered to the other guests at the table.

On my first afternoon we had a meeting with the members of the embryonic Serra. It was held in the bishop's house and he played a very supportive part. It was clear that, were they to obtain their charter, they were assured of the Church's support.

When I retired to my bedroom on the first night I found the suitcase I had left open was now full of very damp clothes. The climate, although not as hot as I had expected, was much more humid than I had ever experienced – even more so than in New Orleans. While I was wondering what, apart from shutting the case, I could do to solve this problem, the door burst open and standing there was my host, the bishop, in shorts and a T-shirt carrying a flit gun. He proceeded to spray the room with disinfectant, apologising for not having done so earlier. This was probably a good idea because the mosquito screen on the window had some very large holes in it.

On one day during my stay I was invited to join the bishop on a visitation of some of his parishes and a convent. He was particularly proud of the convent because it was the first to be opened in Africa. He explained that it was difficult to attract girls to the religious life as remaining single and not having children was contrary to their culture.

On another day the local prospective Serrans arranged for me to be received in audience with Otumfuo Opoku Ware II, King of the Ashanti. We drove to his compound near Kumasi, a very large area enclosed behind a high bamboo fence, where we were asked to wait outside the entrance gate guarded by two warriors in traditional dress. From here we could see peacocks displaying themselves on manicured lawns as the King and his entourage left a substantial, well-built native hut and processed to an even larger hut which we were told was his throne room. The King, in traditional dress, walked under an ornate parasol while he was fanned by servants with two enormous peacock feather fans.

When the His Majesty had entered the throne room we were escorted to join him and invited to sit in very comfortable arm chairs. Attendants entered with incongruous wrought iron and frosted glass trolleys bearing a great variety of spirits and soft drinks. The number of special brandies and whiskeys was remarkable and we were encouraged to take advantage of them. The King introduced himself. He was a barrister who had studied law in London, but had given it up to become tribal ruler when his uncle died When he asked me about myself and discovered I was an architect he informed me that he had originally qualified in surveying and become a building inspector before going to London to study Law. He told us all about the Ashanti tribe and its relation to the government of Ghana, then asked us about London. Finally, after about an hour, he asked me if I would sign his visitors' book. Conducting me to the entrance lobby, he thumbed the pages of an elaborate, leather bound book on a desk until he found what he wanted, then asked me which page I would like to write on. The first page he showed me had the signature of Pope John Paul II on the top of it and nothing else. The second contained only that of Queen Elizabeth II. I wrote my signature and 'President of Serra International' in the book and we left, but I was so overwhelmed that I have no idea now what page I chose.

CHAPTER 36

Serra behind
the Iron Curtain

One of the most exciting sites used by Serra International for its conventions was the Broadmoor Hotel in Colorado Springs. It started life as a casino hotel, catering for those who had achieved success in the silver rush that occurred in the Cheyenne mountains surrounding the hotel. In front of the original building is a large lake, and the path around it gives access to two further hotels built in preference to extending the first. It also provides access to the three golf courses, six tennis courts, eight restaurants and twenty-four shops.

Two of our guests at the convention in 1979 were a bishop and archbishop from Poland, who were invited at the end of the convention to address the board meeting on what they thought of Serra. A story one of them used to illustrate his thinking remains in my memory. He said they were taking a stroll around the lake before dinner one evening when they saw a priest walking ahead of them with one arm around the shoulders of a woman and the other around the shoulders of a man – they were husband and wife. "If Serra managed to introduce that kind of relationship between the priest and laity in Poland," he said, "I would welcome Serra with open arms."

I was in Rome for the Bishops' International Congress on Vocations in May 1981 towards the end of my year of office as international president. While there I was the guest of honour at a meeting of a new Serra group of young engaged couples. During the reception that preceded the lunch I was called to the hotel foyer, where a Monsignor Ryszard Karpinski, who was secretary to the Pontifical Council for Migrants and Itinerants, was waiting to ask me if I was free later in the afternoon to attend a meeting of bishops who were anxious to speak to me. He told me that he could not say who they were but that the topic under discussion would involve vocations. The Italian trustee on the Serra board would also be present. I accepted his invitation and an arrangement was made to collect me from the hotel later.

At the appointed time I was picked up by a black chauffeur-driven limousine, together with the monsignor and the Italian trustee, and driven to a part of town I had not been to before. Before long we were stopped at a road block by the police. After a conversation between a policeman and the monsignor we got out of the car and started to walk. We had not gone far when we were joined by a priest conservatively dressed in a round-brimmed hat and cassock, who introduced himself as the Rector of the Polish seminary. He led the way to the seminary where we were taken into a meeting of the Polish bishops. They were in Rome for their five yearly meeting with the Vatican and the Holy Father, who was also present as he happened to be dining that evening with the students and staff of the seminary.

It was difficult to follow the details of the meeting because the monsignor did not interpret what was being said. Although he spoke Polish, English, and Italian very well, the Italian Serran did not speak English and I did not speak Italian, so it would have been an impossibly difficult task. We just about got the gist of what was being said. They were reflecting on the effect of the creation of the trade union led by Lech Walesa which had emerged from the strike in the Gdansk shipyards, and thinking that it might now be appropriate to challenge the prohibition of lay Catholic organisations, and start such an organisation in Poland. They also thought it would be less controversial if it was seen to be home grown. If designed in a way to enable it to be integrated with an existing international organisation when the time was ripe it would be ideal. To achieve this we were asked whether we would be prepared to visit Poland as tourists. We could then spend some time explaining the concepts of Serra and the existing structure to suitable persons prepared to start Serra in Poland. We both agreed to be available whenever they considered it appropriate.

I did not hear anything further about this proposal, so I assume that 'Solidarity' and the changes started at Gdansk by Lech Walesa were sufficiently effective to make special arrangements for taking Catholic lay organisations into communist countries unnecessary. Italian Serrans have since formed a very effective Serran presence in a large part of the previous Soviet Republic.

I met Monsignor Ryszard several times after this because he became a good friend of Serra in Italy before returning to Poland to become an auxiliary bishop in Lublin. He was occasionally a dinner guest of the Holy Father and the letters with his Christmas cards gave us some interesting insights about His Holiness from the perspective of a fellow Polish prelate.

CHAPTER 37

American Honours

Religion plays an important part in the social and political life of the USA and Serra, as one of the principal Catholic organisations, is treated with great respect. It has a large membership in every State. National and international gatherings provide an ideal opportunity for politicians to address the people, and it is not uncommon for a prominent politician to be invited to such meetings of Serra.

One Serra convention held in Washington was addressed by Dan Quayle when he was vice-president. He entered the room at the head of a procession of twelve FBI agents who kept their beady eyes on us from twelve different positions in the room. On another occasion when, as international president, I was chairing the International convention in Louisville, Kentucky, the governor of the state gave the opening welcome address. At the end of his speech he made me an honorary colonel in the Kentucky army, which is their equivalent of our Freedom of the City. In addition to the freedom of the State, however, I believe I am permitted to wear the pale blue uniform of the confederate army. It also enables me to attend the opening and closing banquets at the annual Kentucky Derby. Some might think that this is more exciting than being able to take one's sheep across London Bridge, which privilege is supposedly conferred by the Freedom of the City of London.

To date I have only presented the prize to the winning jockey of a trotting race at the Louisville track.

During my term as president I was visiting some Serra groups in Mexico and my route included a break of several hours on a Sunday night in Houston. As soon as I was sure of my arrangements I invited Frank Metyko and his wife to come out to the airport for a quiet meal. When I arrived at Houston Frank explained that he had arranged for us to eat at the airport hotel, a short walk away, and that Rita (his wife) was waiting in the restaurant. I followed him out of the terminal and into an adjacent building. I was probably too tired to wonder why we used the lift to a bedroom floor and why we were going down a bedroom corridor. Before I had time to become suspicious I became aware of an abundance of decorations and flags of both our nations around a door ahead. We reached this door, Frank rang the bell and 'God Save the Queen' began playing in the room. Then the door opened and I was greeted by a man who introduced himself as the British Consul. He ushered me in and introduced me to the Mayor of Houston. The Mayor then introduced me to fifteen members of his council who were all crammed into the hotel suite. I was presented with the key and the freedom of the city of Houston, and we all drank champagne.

Although overwhelmed by this honour I was also very tired and conscious that I had to fly to Mexico that night. Dinner, however, had been booked in the penthouse restaurant. This 'quiet dinner' consisted of a table of about ten people, presided over by the British Consul and shared with several of the councillors I had met downstairs. The whole evening was a marvellous experience. When it was over, I was virtually poured onto the plane with my parchment and the key to the city I was leaving.

CHAPTER 38

The Congress of Bishops

I first met Cardinal Baum in 1981 when I was international president of Serra. I was invited to take part with our chief executive, John Donahue, in an international congress of bishops. The Cardinal was Prefect of the Congregation for Education and had called the congress to examine the question of vocations to the priesthood. The number of candidates presenting themselves for priesthood had decreased in many parts of the world, particularly in Europe. We had several opportunities to talk to the Cardinal and, over coffee one morning, he told us how he came to invite Serra to the congress. As a young bishop in America he had got to know the Kansas City Serra Club and realised that there were men in Serra who were capable of using their expertise in business to make a contribution to the various aspects of management in the priesthood. This was the first opportunity he had had of giving us a chance to make that contribution.

I stayed at the Venerable English College with England's two representatives, Bishop Brewer and the Vocation Director for the Diocese of Southwark. The college is a seminary which houses our students for the priesthood studying in Rome, and has done since 1579. It has also a history of hospitality dating back to 1362.

The building was very grand and full of the evidence of

Catholic England's past. The simple entrance on a narrow cobbled street opens into a magnificent twelve-foot corridor hall which runs the full length of the ground floor, past two chapels, a sacristy and refectory, and ends in a glass wall looking out into a magnificent enclosed garden full of mature trees and shrubs. This corridor, the one immediately above it, and the grand staircase contain the pictures of its past history. The names of the many martyrs created by the Reformation and trained here in the college are listed on the wall by the garden entrance – great motivation for our present students.

The Vatican working day did not always fit with the programme of the seminary so some of our meals were taken on our own. This gave me my first chance to spend time with a bishop and to get to understand his role in the Church which was becoming such an important part of my life. We did, however, take some of our meals in the refectory where we sat on benches at long tables with students, staff and other visitors. I remember talking to Monsignor Coughlan, the under secretary at the Council for the Laity, who wanted me to convince Serra to become a member of his council. I knew of the invitation, and the reasons why we had declined it, so I tried to persuade him to alter some of the criteria for membership. Neither of us was successful; Serra is still not a member and it is unlikely that the conditions for membership have changed. The council insisted on control of the constitution and a veto on the choice of president, conditions unacceptable to our American leadership.

I particularly enjoyed dining with my own diocesan students. I had interviewed some of them and it was good to be with them on their journey to priesthood. One evening I was invited to take a glass of wine in one of their rooms, and I still remember one of the problems we discussed because I was party to achieving a solution to it a few years later. It related to the difficulties experienced when students on very different grants lived together. The money they received for pocket money, books and flights varied depending on their diocese.

The congress was inaugurated by Pope John Paul II during mass in St Peter's on Sunday 10th May 1981. The basilica was packed. As the more important of our fellow delegates were participating in the mass our special tickets enabled us to take seats in the front row of the nave. Sitting so close to the altar and the Holy Father would have been exciting under any circumstances, but this was a particularly special occasion and I was very moved. When I received Holy Communion from the Holy Father I was once again overcome with emotion.

The congress was to last seven days and was held in the Vatican Audience Hall, where I had previously attended a papal audience. It is a splendid building designed by the Italian architect, Luigi Nervi, and one of the first to have all its heating and lighting provided by solar panels on the roof. Unlike other very large structures, its 12,000 fixed seats are in one enclosed area. This creates an aura of formality and expectancy that works well for an audience. But I could not visualise how the area could be used for a congress.

When I entered the narthex on the Monday morning this usually empty place had been transformed into a cloakroom, post office, communications centre, meeting and refreshment area. A staircase at either end led up to the simple but comfortable conference facilities above the narthex. The plenary sessions were held in a steeply raked lecture hall with a raised platform on one of the long sides. Here sat the chairman, speaker, secretaries and visiting dignitaries, at a continuous desk capable of accommodating nine people. The rest of us sat in tiers of continuous desks, seating up to 360 participants, normally used for synods and bishops' congresses. I wondered how many of the millions of people attending an audience would be aware that this facility, the nearest the Vatican gets to having a parliament building, is just above their heads.

The congress was composed of members of the Congregation of Education, representatives of the bishops' conferences in the various countries, seminary rectors and vocation directors. The programme was built around five language groups reporting to the whole body of delegates in general sessions. Major presentations by experts were also made at the general sessions. It was interesting to have a copy of the presentation in one language and to be able hear the presentation instantaneously in any of five languages by turning a dial on one's seat. I was surprised at how much it revived one's scrappy knowledge of some of the European languages.

There were about forty-five in the English speaking group, and after the initial gathering of bishops talking to bishops, religious talking to religious, and secular clergy talking to secular clergy, everyone mixed very well and we were all given a chance to speak. It was a very positive exercise, and I enjoyed it greatly.

I also enjoyed the opportunity for sightseeing in Rome during our long lunchtime breaks. The morning session finished at 12.00 pm and the afternoon session started at 4.00 pm. There was much to see on the route between the Vatican and the English College. On the Wednesday I had to make some important telephone calls and was late setting off for the afternoon session. When I arrived at St Peter's the area inside the colonnade was full of pilgrims at the end of an audience. I was walking deliberately slowly behind the seating in the square, observing the Holy Father as he toured the aisles between the seats in his 'popemobile'. I had been watching him for about five minutes when I heard the shots. I could not see much, because he was only halfway through the pilgrims. I could only see the heads of the men surrounding the pope-mobile. They started to run in the direction of Porta Angelica. The audience, which filled most of the square, fell silent for several minutes. Most could have seen only the little I had seen, but they would all have heard the shots. Then there was an eruption of sound as they began asking each other what had happened. They remained where they stood, no doubt wondering whether the Holy Father was safe, for the length of time it took me to leave the square.

On my walk back to the congress my thoughts were very mixed. I had already got to know him, I had spoken to him and received Communion from him. I had grown very fond of him and now he might be dead or dying. There was nothing I could do, however, except pray that he was unhurt.

The congress had already heard about the shooting, but no details were known. Before we left that evening, we learned through those of our fellow delegates who had direct links with the Vatican that the Pontiff had been shot four times: two wounds were in the arm and hand respectively and were not dangerous; two shots, however, had entered the stomach and were serious. The following morning we learnt from the Gemelli Hospital, where he had been taken, that operations to the stomach had been successful and there was a good prospect of his making a full recovery. By the conclusion of the congress the Holy Father was out of danger.

Some sixteen years later, the next bishops' congress was held. It was decided that the work of the congress could be more effective if the world were divided into regions, in recognition of the fact that the situation in those parts of the developing world where there were large numbers of novices and seminarians was very different from those places suffering from a shortage of priests. I was invited to participate in the

European Bishops' Congress, which took place in the Vatican in May, 1997. Almost none of those present had been to the previous meeting. This one was less formal and more intense but, nevertheless, reached much the same conclusion as its predecessor as to the paucity of vocations, the only difference being that society had become even more secular and many of the 1981 decisions had either not been followed or were found to have been less effective than expected. There was a commitment to proclaiming the concept of active Catholicism as being in itself a vocation, on the basis that if 'vocation' in its general sense were promoted, the special vocations to the ordained ministry or the religious life would follow.

The Eastern Regional Congress was held in conjunction with the Serra International Convention in Bangkok, Thailand, in June, 2005 and although I did not participate in their discussions many of the presentations were made to both groups. The differences between the Eastern and European congresses were striking. Our problems were due to falling numbers. The Churches in India, China, Indonesia, Thailand and the Philippines were all growing fast, and most of their problems related to growth accompanied by lack of finance. Some of them were also suffering from Islamic persecution, a problem which, sadly, has become more acute in recent times.

CHAPTER 39

The mass at Wembley with Pope John Paul II

Late in December 1980 I was having dinner in my flat with Monsignor Ralph Brown, the Vicar General of our diocese of Westminster. One of the topics we discussed was his recent appointment as National Coordinator of the visit of Pope John Paul II to England in 1982. I told him that I would like to be involved in some way. I was hoping he might consider me for the role of designer of the environment for one of the masses. However, he told me that no decisions had yet been made. Sometime in the spring of 1981 the venues in the various parts of the country, and the architects involved, were announced. I was disappointed to find that I was not included. The Westminster Diocese was to share a mass with the other southern dioceses, and the venue chosen was Richmond Park. The architect was Ron Tallon of Scott Tallon, the Irish practice that designed the very successful environment for the papal mass in Phoenix Park, Dublin.

The arrangements for Richmond were well developed before the police decided that they could not secure the park against possible disturbance. They wanted the Church to cancel the event or try and find a totally enclosed area. Accordingly, the dioceses decided to move the mass to Wembley Stadium.

Wembley was known for this kind of event because it had been the site for the public mass for a congregation of 85,000 at the anniversary congress of the Restoration of the Catholic Hierarchy in 1950. On that occasion, my brother and I had carried the two poles of a banner in front of one of the groups of youths gathered on the pitch for a historical pageant that had preceded the mass.

The contract for the use of Wembley was signed less than nine months before the visit. But to avoid the criticism aroused by the original choice of an Irish architectural practice, the dioceses took advantage of the change of venue to hold a competition for the architect. The Irish practice was to be retained as adviser. Each of the nine southern dioceses were asked to invite one architect and I believe that Monsignor Ralph added a further three to make twelve, of which mine was one. I received my first indication that we were included by letter on Christmas Eve. I opened it just before our guests were due to arrive for a Christmas drink with the partners and staff. We were given just a little over two weeks to prepare the drawings and a model. The presentation was to be on the 12th of January. After very few minutes' thought I telephoned Wembley Stadium and was lucky enough to find someone senior enough to allow us to start our survey on Tuesday the 29th of December. This was the first day after the bank holiday, and exactly five months before the event on the 29th May. It was normal for me to say a few words after the office Christmas lunch so I took the opportunity to tell my colleagues and staff about the competition. I explained how I had taken advantage of receiving the invitation before the holidays and asked for a volunteer to help me with the survey. Peter Baker offered to give up part of his holiday and I offered him the chance to stay on the project if we won.

Wembley was able to give us sufficient copies of the

drawings of the stadium and the surrounding car park for us to send some off to the model maker. This enabled him to start building the background to our design. I then prepared two schemes and invited the partners and staff to help me decide on which one we should base our entry. There was just sufficient time for the maker to finish the model and for us to finish the design drawings. We worked fifteen hours a day and were very tired by the time we arrived at Archbishop's House for the presentation. I have no clear impression of how the scheme was received. I was, however, reasonably, confident that we had a good chance.

Because the time for us to prepare our scheme was so short I expected to hear the result the following day. When I had heard nothing by the weekend, I began to think we must have lost. I had certainly given up any possibility of winning when, over two weeks later, I received the call from Monsignor Ralph telling me we had won. My delight was mixed with amazement at how long they had taken to reach a decision. I spent most of the call feeling annoyed at the loss of twenty per cent of the time available, but I was particularly pleased to find that we had beaten the internationally known practice of Ove Arup into second place.

I had no time to go to tender so I chose a shop-fitting contractor, W. S. Try, who had proved to me in the past that they could do this type of work within the proposed programme. I allowed them to choose the sub-contractors with only one caveat: that each of the firms involved would have a responsible director in charge of its contract, willing to be resident in the hotel adjoining the stadium for the duration the contract was on site.

Wembley presented us with several problems. The greatest was the time we were allowed on site: from midnight on Wednesday till 8.00 am the following Saturday – some fifty-six hours. This was to allow for the possibility of a replay of the Saturday Cup Final – and, of course, there was a replay. Wembley was not large enough for the predicted congregation of over 100,000, so we would need to have people on the pitch and in the car parks outside the stadium. The pitch would have to be covered in such a way as to prevent condensation affecting the grass. The people in the car park would require television on large screens and, to satisfy the police, they would have to be enclosed in pens created by security fencing, and this fencing would have to be dismantled for the Sunday market by 6.00 am the morning after the event.

The protection of the dog track running around the perimeter of the pitch was even more important than the pitch. Much of Wembley's income came from televising dog racing on this track. It would have to be treated or covered in order to avoid being damaged by the mobile cranes and other heavy vehicles.

The existing toilet facilities were intended for a predominantly male audience using the stadium for a maximum of three hours. We had to provide for a much larger proportion of women and children, and all for the best part of a day.

The existing sound system was designed not to be heard on the pitch, so additional systems would be required.

We managed to arrange two meetings of everyone responsible for the mass at the stadium. They were happy occasions that were easy to chair but it was necessary to include some forty people to cover the many different interests: the stadium managers, liturgy, MCs, vestments, communion hosts and wine, musicians, choir, souvenir and mass books, tickets, stewards, police, furniture and carpet hire, insurance, contractors and sub-contractors. Not surprisingly, most of the detail was decided outside the meetings.

There were only three issues that caused any real concern:

whether or not there should be a collection; when the contractors should hand over to the choir and musicians; and where the statue of Our Lady of Walsingham should be located.

It was decided that there would be a collection, and we made provision for collectors and a dozen volunteer bank staff with their counting machines, but the result was disappointing: we collected less than 40 pence per adult present.

The choir and musicians won. They wanted to have a leisurely break between their rehearsal and rehearsing with the congregation. They took possession at 8.00 am for the mass at 4.00 pm, which used up 12.5 per cent of the total preparation time. Had they been prepared to have their own rehearsal while we were still working, or while the people were coming into the stadium we could have had a significant addition to our fifty-six hours.

The discussions on the site for the statue of our Lady of Walsingham were more difficult. It was to be brought up from Walsingham in procession and the Walsingham Association was keen to have it placed in a prominent position on the presbyterium. The liturgists were of the opinion that the presbyterium was an inappropriate place for the statue of Our Lady during mass. I was of the opinion that the statue, less than eighteen inches tall would be lost on the presbyterium. Very few people would be able to see a statue barely two feet tall. Our solution, reluctantly accepted by both parties was to sacrifice a significant piece of standing area on the front terrace adjoining the presbyterium. This would be filled with flowers surrounding a plinth on which the statue would repose. We did not see the statue arrive but a study of the many photographs of the event shows nothing in the large bed of flowers, and the statue on the altar during the mass – a good example of *sensus fidelium*.

I believe that most of our competitors chose to have the

presbyterium on the pitch or at the end opposite the players' entrance. We, however, decided to place it opposite the centre line and in the position of the Royal Box. It was to start about halfway up the stands and cross over the dog track to steps on the edge of the pitch. The height was just sufficient for the Holy Father to pass under it in his popemobile.

The platform was composed of eight prefabricated steel units each eight feet wide and sixty feet long which could be carried on long, low loading vehicles. Structural engineer Jim Daly, a Serran friend of mine, had some difficulty in justifying the structure because of the weakness of the terraces to carry the end of the platform. After some negotiation we managed to get Wembley to allow us access to the stadium for an extra full day at the beginning of May, which enabled the contractor to drive concrete piles through the terraces to solid ground. The front end of our platform was carried on foundations below the shingle in the border between pitch and track which we poured during the same day. We also used that day to give the drivers a chance to practise driving the low loaders backwards round the dog track, and to see whether two small mobile cranes could erect the platform sections. We hoped this would give us a good idea of how long the operation would take. However, by the time the sections were in place we realised the time taken was much greater than we had anticipated. In subsequent negotiations with the sub-contractor we found that, unbeknownst to him, the erecting gang had discovered that they were eligible for a bonus payment the size of which would be directly related to how much faster they could erect it on the day. They had, therefore, taken their time.

This project brought the practice much publicity, not merely because of the amount of work we had to do in a week, but because the mass was to take place one week after the FA Cup Final; when there was a replay, the publicity was even more intense. Much of our time was taken up with press and television interviews. I was even invited to have lunch with the president of our professional body at the Royal Institute of British Architects, but I don't remember it bringing in more commissions.

The day I presented the budget to Cardinal Hume it had reached £300,000. He was concerned but disinclined to say more than that we should attempt to make any possible savings. Then he noticed the £30,000 allowed for the cross and said he could not be responsible for spending that kind of money on a cross. I explained that our design was dependent on the cross being large enough to provide a spiritual background to the event. It was fifty-six feet high and two feet wide. Bishop Tom McMahon, who was responsible for the liturgy for Wembley, was also present and leant his support to my argument. After much discussion, it was agreed that we could proceed with the cross if Bishop McMahon was satisfied we had got the price down to an acceptable level. After much thought and some experimenting in the office we came up with a design that could be installed for less than £10,000 and the bishop was satisfied. It was based on two crosses of woven plastic sail cloth stretched on wire cables and fixed, one cross eighteen inches in front of the other. With the lighting, necessary under the roof to the stands, focused accurately, the cross appeared solid. The cables were easily fixed at its base but the top was more difficult. In the end we used a volunteer on a bosun's chair to tie the ends of the cross bar and the top of the cross to the roof structure of the stands. Even though we had the obligatory three men controlling the stabilising ropes, the sight of a man sitting on a seat such as you find on a child's swing and controlling his own height and movement more than fifty feet off the ground was terrifying

Wembley gave us the twelve tickets for the FA Cup Final replay that we had asked for, which allowed twelve strong men to remove the seats from the area of stands to be covered by our platform. The moment the occupants got up to applaud the end of the match the men would start to undo the seat fixings. This would have given us a two hour advantage over our contract entry time. We were also given consent after the players had left the pitch for a forklift truck to bring in the first load of materials to cover the pitch. Unfortunately, the man chosen for this job had had more than a few drinks and become a little the worse for wear. As a result, he managed to ram his forklift vehicle into the side wall of the players' tunnel. By the time the ambulance had taken him out through the tunnel and our first vehicles could enter the stadium, the time gained was minimal.

When the contract started on site the atmosphere created by the pressure of having to work to such a tight deadline was amazing. Everyone gave of their best, aided by the presence of their directors who laid on first class food and drink. This is particularly important on a contract that runs without stopping. Many of the men had almost no rest for the length of their part of the contract. The trades were more helpful to each other in resolving problems than is usual, and rather more risks were taken. For example, the metal bands tying up the bundles of plywood for covering the pitch were not individually cut. The cranes picked up the sheets, still tied together in bundles, from the lorries. The bundles strained against the holding cables and caused the bands to burst open and fly all over the place. This was dangerous, but made the job much quicker. When the mobile cranes were lifting the platform sections they were very clearly working very close to their maximum capacity and there were times when one could see more than two of their wheels off the ground.

The shortage of time on site, however, had advantages. The surveyor responsible for inspecting the structure was unhappy with the absence of handrails to the altar steps. We said we would put some in, but we did not tell him that we were due to finish the following morning, and the chance of his returning the same day was unlikely.

Although the erection of the platform with its built in seating and furniture took time, the greatest proportion of time was spent on setting out 650 seats on the pitch for the clergy, and placing on tables 60 chalices and 584 ciboria for the 100,000 communicants, to say nothing of the 400 buckets for the collection, laying miles of carpet, providing additional loos, and building the miles of secure fencing to the people pens for the pitch and car parks. There were also some special features such as providing a secure helipad in an adjoining school, hoisting an organ up into the area set aside for the orchestra and choir at the back of the terraces, and converting one of the players' dressing areas into the room where the Holy Father would robe for mass. In the event he was there for some time, waiting for his vestments to arrive from Wimbledon. He had been with the Archbishop at Canterbury in the morning, where he had had no need of vestments. The requirement for vestments in the afternoon seemed to have been forgotten and it required urgent phone calls to rectify the situation. This slight delay enabled me to explain the significance of the area he occupied and he was particularly pleased to hear that his entry into the stadium would be through the players' tunnel.

We did finish on time and my only regret was that we had had no time to stretch the carpet, at least on the presbyterium. It had looked good at about midnight but the early morning dew had created significant ripples on its surface. It improved as the sun came up and you certainly can't see it in the photographs. I gave all the workers a ten hour rest break, and I had my first rest since the five hours I had snatched on Thursday night. I found a nice spot on some uncovered grass under the steps to the presbyterium, where I savoured the feeling of relief that all had gone well and managed to get some sleep during the choir practice before the crowd started to enter the stadium. The atmosphere was very festive and alive with expectancy as people ate their hot dogs, sandwiches or ice-cream. Taking advantage of my pass, which allowed me to go anywhere, to check on how the various stewards were coping with the facilities we had provided, I received the assurance of Father Eddie Matthews and his MCs that everything was in order on the presbyterium. I met the police officer we had asked to look after the rather special old and valuable sacred vessels. He had exchanged his uniform for a cassock and cotta to enable him to move more freely around the sacred area.

The only responsibility I had during the mass itself was to be the last in the line of those receiving communion from the Holy Father. This would enable the MC assisting the Holy Father to know when the number of communicants agreed with the Vatican organiser of the event, Archbishop Marcinkus, had received communion. When I joined the line of the other nineteen communicants and started to climb the steps of the presbyterium, I became aware that the stewards were not preventing others from joining on behind me. The Holy Father carried on giving communion to these extra communicants until the MC eventually contrived to relieve him of the ciborium and escort him back to the papal chair designed for His Holiness. I saw this same chair a few months ago in the sacristy at the Church of Our Lady of Victories in High Street, Kensington – an indication of how reluctant we can be to destroy souvenirs of important events. After the communion, I went back to my spot under the steps, but the excellent singing of such a large congregation kept me awake, although I did manage to have a good rest. After the mass I joined our policeman in keeping watch on the presbyterium and surrounding areas to make sure nobody took the communion ciborium, chairs or pieces of the hired carpet, etc. as souvenirs.

Before the last of the crowds had left the stadium we were beginning to take everything down, as we had to be clear before the first vehicles arrived to set up for the market in the car parks the following morning.

The platform sections were taken to their spare piece of land at the back of the stadium but before we took them away I contacted Wembley administration to suggest they might like to purchase them because the sections could be fixed to our new foundations and create a stage for the many concerts which are held in the stadium each year. It would have had the advantage of vibrating less than the scaffolding presently used and we had proved that it could be erected in less than two days. Wembley, however, were not interested. The pop groups were presently hiring the stadium for at least a week to erect their scaffolding, and our arrangement would only have reduced Wembley's income.

There was another reason for contacting Wembley after the event: to make arrangements for repairing the pitch's automatic watering system – it must have been damaged by the load we had placed on it. This could have resulted in a substantial surcharge had we not been helped by the local Fire Brigade. They watered the grass with one of their tenders, entirely free of charge, throughout the week it took us to repair the leaks.

CHAPTER 40

The Synods

In 1986 major Catholic organisations were asked to select representatives to attend the VIIth Synod 'ON THE VOCATION AND THE MISSION OF THE LAY FAITHFUL IN THE CHURCH AND IN THE WORLD', but the Vatican subsequently had second thoughts and decided to limit the number of the laity at the synod. Those originally invited would attend a preparatory council led by some of the synod Fathers. These Fathers, together with a considerably reduced number of lay people, would represent the views of the laity. I attended the council, which was held in a large conference centre at Rocca Di Papa up in the Alban Hills, fiftteen miles south of Rome. I was not chosen to attend the synod.

It was a privilege to be part of the first opportunity the laity had had to make a contribution at the highest level of the church. Unfortunately, conservatives and liberals were sharply divided in their opinions and neither showed much understanding of, or sympathy for, the other's point of view. There was also little understanding of the different approaches which characterised different cultures. I was particularly surprised at the strength of support for pre-Vatican II liturgy, and was reminded of Cardinal Basil Hume's opinion that it would take a century for Vatican II to be fully accepted.

The synod was going to have difficultly in representing the universality of our church in any progress it hoped to make.

On the last day I decided to leave the conference centre at lunchtime. I wanted to go for a walk in the hope of finding a café and a glass of wine. On the way out I met Cardinal Basil Hume, enjoying a stroll and a cigarette. He was chairing one of the French language groups, and was clearly unhappy. He felt that the organisers should have realised that being able to speak French as a second language was not sufficient to equip one for controlling a difficult debate in that language. I also got the impression that he was not convinced of the value of the exercise. When I reached the café for which I was aiming, I met Paddy Linehan whom I knew slightly and who has since became a member of my Catenian Circle. Paddy was representing Catholic doctors at another conference in Rome.

The conference centre was not residential so I stayed at the Villa Palazzola, a short walk away, where our Rome Seminary students used to stay in the summer to escape the heat of the city. Visitors to Rome who seek a place of peace and quiet can enjoy its cloisters and gardens, and maybe even the swimming pool. Palazzola is perched high up on the sides of a cliff overlooking Lake Albano and has a wonderful view across the lake to Castel Gandolfo, the Pope's summer retreat, where I have been lucky enough to attend a general audience with the Pontiff.

My disappointment at losing a chance to see a synod in action was resolved in the late summer of 1990 when I received a telephone call from Archbishop Luigi Barbarito, the Papal Nuncio in England. He asked me whether I was in a position to accept an invitation from the Holy Father to be an auditor at the VIIIth Synod in October 'ON THE FORMATION OF PRIESTS IN THE CIRCUMSTANCES OF THE PRESENT DAY'. Without thinking about how I could take a whole month off from the practice at a time of recession, I said "Yes". I was not going to miss this opportunity to be part of the most senior of all the decision making bodies in the Church. Popes through the ages had called synods of bishops to help them make particular decisions, and the Second Vatican Council had decreed henceforth that they should meet every four years to study a specific subject.

At the beginning of September my invitation arrived and my role was defined as someone with a particular expertise who may take an active part in the proceedings but who is not a member of the synod and may not vote on motions. I was provided with a great number of documents to study, among them the concluding document of the 1981 Congress on Vocations that I had attended, and told I could apply for financial assistance and free accommodation at the Istituto Ravasco if I needed them.

Having sent the biographical and security information, together with the photographs requested, I endeavoured to obtain accommodation at the Venerable English College, of which I am a 'Friend', but they were full with the entourage of the two bishops representing our Church in England and Wales. Archbishop Worlock and Bishop Brewer had brought with them the staff they needed to help run their dioceses from Rome and to prepare their presentations.

The Istituto Ravasco was a convent offering some fifty modern, single en suite rooms for the use of people having business with the Vatican. The hard, narrow bed – and even narrower shower room – gave my six foot, four inch frame several problems, and there was no bar in which to drown my sorrows. There was, however, a beautiful chapel, where our day began at 6.30 am, singing lauds with the nuns before mass – the perfect start for the experience to come.

My first full day in Rome was Sunday 30th September. I

went to St Peter's for the opening mass. The lay people and the religious were seated in the front two rows of a segment of the horseshoe of clergy. It was very impressive to see such a large proportion of the world's hierarchy saying mass with the Holy Father. The gathering was greatly enhanced by the golden vestments and mitres of the patriarchs. At the offertory, I and the lay secretary to the African Conference of Bishops presented the bread and wine to the Holy Father, and he thanked us for giving up our time for the synod.

The following day the fifteen auditors staying at the Istituto were taken by bus to the Nervi Synod Hall, a quarter of an hour's drive away. As I approached the narthex the Swiss Guard saluted; inside, the security men checked my identity and presented me with my security pass and a fine red brief case. These were each embossed with 'The VIII General Synod' and the Vatican coat of arms. The lockable case was filled with working documents, lists of participants, a most beautiful booklet containing the divine office for the month, and a timetable. Our working day consisted of a general session from 9.00 am until 10.30 am, a coffee break, another general session from 11.00 am till 12.30 pm, followed by the lunch break which lasted until 4.30 when we were expected to return and take coffee before attending the working groups in our own language from 5.00 pm until 7.00 pm.

In the narthex I was able to purchase photographs of myself at the previous day's mass, and collect a translation of the Holy Father's homily in my own personal pigeon hole. I could also collect newly printed books publishers wanted us to promote, take advantage of the free facilities of the temporary Vatican post office and enjoy some fairly elaborate refreshments.

I had the choice of drinking coffee with any one of the six patriarchs, forty-seven cardinals, over 168 archbishops and bishops representing ninety-seven countries, and seventeen generals of religious orders who made up the membership of the synod, to say nothing of the forty-nine rectors, professors, spiritual directors, directors of vocation, four laymen, and three laywomen auditors.

I knew the other Serrans: Giuliano Rizzerio, president of Italian Serra, and Henry Nelson, the Ghanaian Secretary of the Pan African Laity Conference, who had been with me at the congress on vocations. Other friends I had made at that conference were Cardinal Baum, Bishop John Onaiyekan from Nigeria and Fathers Kim Suela and Francis Bonnici, Vocation Directors for the Philippines and Malta respectively. I also knew Archbishop Derek Worlock and Bishop John Brewer, representing England and Wales, and the Cardinals Joseph Bernadin and James Hickey from Serra in the States. There were a few other bishops and priests whom I had met over the years, travelling in different countries for Serra, and that helped to start conversations. It was not until we had broken down into the thirteen language groups that I got to know new people. By the end of the synod we had become a great Christian family.

At five to nine the bell called us to take our prearranged positions in the Synod Hall for the sung morning office in Latin. This was led by the Holy Father from the dais, as indeed it was on most days. He attended the whole of twenty-seven of the thirty half-day plenary sessions, and hypnotised everybody with his magnetic personality. His wonderfully articulate hand movements eloquently augmented his comments at the end of the presentations. He was able to show pleasure, agreement, support and concern without saying a word.

At our first break for coffee on the first day I explained to Cardinal Baum that I was an architect and anxious to use the long four-hour lunch breaks constructively. I asked him if it was possible to see those parts of the Vatican not normally open to the public. He said he thought that would be possible, and offered to make an appointment with the president of the Vatican City, Archbishop Paul Marcinkus, "whom you will probably not have heard of." I explained that I had met him before and that many in my country knew of him through the press coverage of his involvement with Banco Ambrosiano.*

The following morning Cardinal Baum told me that he had arranged for me to have coffee with Archbishop Marcinkus, so I walked round to his office. He welcomed me warmly, saying that he was pleased to be able to arrange for me to see the Vatican. He had arranged for me to meet the Technical Director of Vatican City the following day. Coffee arrived and we had it sitting at his desk, which he explained was very special because it had belonged to Pope Pius X. He was particularly interested in how I had been chosen as an auditor, which gave me the opportunity to tell him about Serra and my work with interviewing candidates for the priesthood. The next day I visited the Technical Director. He spoke only a little English but with the help of an interpreter he explained that I would be better served by his deputy, who had been a prisoner of war in my country, married an English girl, and spoke the language well. I was to meet him 'tomorrow'.

I was beginning to wonder if I was ever going to get inside the Vatican when, over coffee the following day, I was presented with a programme of visits with the various heads of department, plus the offer of his Mercedes and driver to take me to the various locations. This, he said was not on account of the distance but for security. It was not practical for me to be wandering around the Vatican alone, and this way the driver could introduce me to the heads of the departments.

Some of the things I saw were open to the public, but I was seeing them under ideal conditions, and with the best of guides. I visited the major rooms in the Vatican palace, the main exhibitions, the observatory, railway station, heliport, the papal gardens, the palace for non-catholic clergy, the cemetery, the stamp and coin collections, the area of the Roman cemetery and mausolea below the crypt in St Peter's and, most exciting of all, the Sistine Chapel, where I was allowed to climb the scaffolding and watch the restorers working on the top of the end wall. These experiences made my attendance at the Synod that much more special, and the break in the middle of the day was every bit as refreshing as taking a siesta.

The process of the Synod must fascinate the layman accustomed to the usual methods of decision making in the temporal world. We spent the first eleven days listening, with the aid of excellent simultaneous translation, to twenty-minute presentations by the auditors and eight-minute interventions by members of the synod on various aspects of the particular topic. These contributions were assisted by a working document previously prepared by the synod secretariat and based on worldwide consultation.

At the end of two weeks the secretariat produced a working document based on the plenary sessions and the recorded deliberations of the thirteen working groups into which we had been divided. This document was then returned to the working groups, who produced their own version of the document. After three days the discussion groups returned to the Synod Hall to be influenced by hearing the reports of the other groups, before proceeding to revise their own reports and convert them into a series of propositions in Latin. This was not quite as difficult as it sounds. Most people could, in the light of the previous discussions, read and understand Latin and there were enough people present who could translate into Latin what each group wanted to say.

The reporting secretaries of the thirteen working groups were then given twenty-four hours (and midnight oil) to convert all their deliberations into a total of forty-one propositions representing the combined views of all thirteen groups. These were then taken back to the groups to ensure the propositions accurately reflected their views, then used by the reporting secretaries to produce the conclusive forty-one propositions of the synod. It was these propositions that formed the basis of the Holy Father's 'Apostolic Exhortation'.

It was fascinating to witness the mood swings among the participants as the process gathered momentum. They varied from excitement and satisfaction to frustration and depression. The first two were normally felt whenever our language group finalised a stage, and the latter two when our work was amalgamated with the work of other groups. The worst depression came with the reading of the first draft of the propositions, but when these were altered by the final amendments the great majority appeared to be satisfied with their work, and the lowest vote received for any proposition was 190 out of 229. The second lowest was 204, and 27 of the propositions received over 220 votes: a truly convincing endorsement.

These propositions related to the discernment of vocations, the identity of the priest, pre-seminary, seminary and post seminary formation, the training of formation personnel, and the ministry of the priest in the circumstances of the present day.

The Synod general sessions also provided an opportunity for bishops of the Eastern European countries, who were attending for the first time, to tell us something of their past sufferings and the resurgence of the church in their countries. Many of these bishops had themselves spent years in prison and their moving interventions acted as a great stimulant to the proceedings.

Time was also given to receiving reports on decisions made

at past synods, and to executing certain matters requiring the presence of bishops from several countries. At this synod there was a formal presentation of the Canon Law for Eastern Churches, and reports by the presidents of the commissions tasked with preparing the new universal catechism and the studies on the theological and juridical status of bishops' conferences.

Much of the work of the synod was carried out during the coffee breaks and at receptions held in the various national seminaries in Rome. It was exciting to be part of discussions that would influence life in our church for years to come and to meet the famous and those destined to become famous. At a reception at the Venerable English College I first met Bishop Cahal Daly who was informed during the synod that he was to be made Cardinal Primate of all Ireland.

On one of the Sundays we were all requested to attend a mass concelebrated in the square in front of St Peter's to announce the beatification of Giuseppe Allamano. The presence of the synod Fathers in colourful choir dress made it another very special occasion. A portrait of the beatified cleric had been embroidered on a large banner and hung from one of the balconies on the front of St Peter's. The identity passes we had been given allowed access to almost everywhere in Vatican City, so I chose to see the mass from the roof of one of the side wings of the Vatican palace. It is only some twenty feet above the square and the view of the service and those attending was spectacular.

The last Saturday evening was spent in the presence of the Holy Father at a televised concert for 10,000 in the audience hall. On the last day he celebrated mass in St Peter's, which officially concluded the synod. The service was followed by a 'Convivium' (lunch) where the Holy Father said farewell to us all.

One might have thought that being in the presence of the Pope on so many occasions would have lessened the impact he had on us but that was certainly not the case. At the end of every morning he was with us he would leave the plenary session via the staircase at the far end of the narthex. By the time he got into his open-topped car at the bottom of the staircase his route through the narthex would be lined with the synod participants, who clapped and cheered him all the way to the entrance at the other end of the narthex.

We were allocated numbered seats in the raked, lecture-style plenary hall. This made it possible for us to receive messages from people who knew our seat position. Every morning one of the Holy Father's two secretaries would enter during a break between speakers and, starting at the bottom of the raked tiers, hand a batch of envelopes to the person at the end of the row. Rumour had it that these contained invitations for a meal with His Holiness. Rumour gave no indication, however, as to whether we would *all* receive an invitation or whether the invitation would be to an intimate evening meal or a larger luncheon. Whenever a secretary began handing out the envelopes the talking stopped and you could hear the proverbial pin drop until the last envelope had been received. I was very excited when a batch of envelopes passed to me contained one with my name on it and thrilled when I found it contained an invitation to dinner that evening. These dinners took placed in the papal apartment and were limited to nine guests.

That evening I left the synod with Henry Nelson, the only person I had found to be a fellow guest, and walked across St Peter's square to the bronze door of the Apostolic Palace. We showed our invitations to the Swiss Guard in the hall of the Scala Regia, Bernini's famous perspectival staircase. St Peter's and the Vatican join at an obtuse angle but the staircase and hall have been designed to make both appear to be in the same plane. Following the instructions to the lift, we ascended to the third floor and found ourselves in a corner of the gallery around a central atrium. The Swiss Guard at the lift entrance indicated a very ordinary door in a very ordinary wall on one side of the atrium and told us to ring the bell. It was opened by one of the secretaries who took our briefcases; we then joined the other guests. Here we remained until everyone arrived. We were then taken into the adjoining library, where Heads of State are received in private audiences. We introduced ourselves to the Holy Father and photographs were taken of the group. Just then we were joined by the two American Seminary rectors who had arrived late. The Holy Father stopped the photographer leaving and we posed for a further set of photographs.

After that, Pope John Paul led us into the private part of the papal apartment where we entered his very small private chapel in which he said grace before meals. I was last in and stood just inside the door. On his way out the Holy Father took my arm and we led the others into his private dining room where his two secretaries joined us. The Holy Father seated the only other layman present, Henry Nelson, on his left and myself on his right. The meal was simple. We were told the soup was Polish, but I was not concentrating on the food. I think the main course was roast meat of some sort and two vegetables. I do remember that we finished with fresh fruit, and that the Holy Father drank only half his glass of wine before having it topped up with water. I also noticed he wore white protective linen covers to the lower arms of his white cassock.

Our fellow guests were English speaking rectors of seminaries or Directors of Vocations from the USA, The Philippines, Korea, Malta and Nigeria. The conversation never slowed down, the Holy Father only needing help with the odd word here and there. In the first part of the evening he conversed with each of us in turn about his visit to our respective countries; then we discussed the work of the synod. He was happy to answer questions, and one struck me as especially worthy of note. He was asked why he appeared to be supportive of groups like Opus Dei and the Neocatechumenate, and he said that until we understood how to imbue the main body of the Church with the commitment and piety that these groups had in large measure we ignored them at our peril.

The evening ended as it had started – in the chapel, saying grace after the meal. It had not lasted very long, but the experience of being in the close presence of a future saint and the most inspiring image of priesthood I have been privileged to meet will motivate me in Serra for the rest of my life.

★ See footnote to Chapter 24.

CHAPTER 41

Religious Knighthoods

The Equestrian Order of the Holy Sepulchre

Frank Lloyd, who had introduced me to Serra, also proposed me for admission to The Equestrian Order of the Holy Sepulchre. I was invested by Archbishop Cyril Cowderoy in Southwark Cathedral in 1971. Peter Rigby and Frans van den Berg were my sponsors.

The Order was created in 1099 to protect the Church of the Holy Sepulchre in Jerusalem and existed in various forms in different parts of the world until 1928 when it was reformed with its present structure. It was re-established in England in 1954. Its present purpose is to support, by the presence and finance of its members, the Holy Places and the Christians in the Holy Land.

When I joined there were only between fifty and sixty knights and dames in the whole of the British Isles. It was a homogeneous group of people. The fact that it was open to bishops, priests, lay men and women, married and single, and that we wore elaborate cloaks, regalia and headgear, as well as having a very positive purpose, made it attractive to our Catholic friends and that is why it grew quickly. After a few years our Lieutenancy held special investitures in Scotland and Ireland, and these investitures were the beginning of the separate Lieutenancies in those countries. Even after the Scots and Irish had left us we numbered over 400 members. Today we are over 600 in England.

The next stage in our growth was to divide England into Sections. The North of England was the first to put on events of its own, and others soon followed. When most of the country was covered the National Council made it mandatory for everyone to be in a Section. Those in the Westminster diocese, who had not chosen to set up a Section of their own, were assigned to the East Anglia Section. The travelling that this entailed was unreasonable, so we gave in and created the Westminster Section. I had been the lay MC of the English Lieutenancy for fourteen years when it was decided that that was long enough and I was made president of the new Westminster Section, an office I held for a further ten years.

The Order is a properly religious chivalric Order, not an honorific one, and the vigil and investiture ceremony impose on the new knight the duty to be an exemplary Christian. The acceptance of the sword and the words that go with it certainly do much to strengthen one's resolve to be a better Christian, and the association with disadvantaged people in the Holy Land serves as a constant reminder of the needs of others.

The Order gave me the opportunity to make pilgrimages to the Holy Land. The first time I entered Palestine from Jordan was in the early 1970s, on the day after a Jewish holiday. The border was closed for the holiday and a large number of people were waiting to cross. Those on foot were waiting in an open compound without shelter from the sun; we were fortunate to be in our air conditioned coach. In an attempt to increase our chance of crossing the frontier that day we persuaded Bishop Henderson to wear his full choir dress. He then accompanied our courier into the office to see the border officials. This must have helped us to get permission to proceed to the 'No Man's Land' between the two states. At the halfway point we had to get off the coach and sit on a bench under the watchful eyes of a young Israeli soldier who pointed his rifle at us the whole time. When officials had finished searching the coach, our driver and guide were replaced by Israeli equivalents and we were allowed to proceed to the customs building. Here we were strip-searched and the contents of our cases thoroughly examined before being X-rayed. While this took place an Israeli soldier sat on a table in a relaxed manner, casually pointing a gun in our direction. I found this much more frightening than if he had been alert.

Our pilgrimage was without incident, however, and our visits to the Holy Places, hitherto known only from the bible, were enhanced by that knowledge. Seeing and being in these places gives the bible, and particularly the readings at mass, much more meaning and resonance. I am sure different people are moved by different places, but my strongest images are of the very green stretch of the Jordan where Our Lord was baptised, and the solemn procession into the church of the Holy Sepulchre. The most important non-biblical experiences for me were the covered market in Jerusalem and our audience with the Latin Patriarch of Jerusalem, who presented me with my pilgrim's shell.

We ended the pilgrimage with a visit to Petra which proved more exciting and impressive than the photographs one has seen. We travelled through the desert on a tarmacadam strip, the only things to be seen for miles being sand, goats, sheep and the occasional Bedouin encampment. Petra itself was still only a car park, with donkeys waiting to be hired and a café carved out of the mountain surrounding the hidden city. It is only when you are helped onto a donkey that you notice the cleft in the rock through which you must travel. It takes about twenty minutes before you can see anything through the opening at the end of the passage. What you eventually do see is magnificent and as you get closer and more of the temple is revealed one's excitement mounts. The city is much larger and better preserved than I had expected. Almost all the original buildings are carved out of the rock which surrounds this vast open area.

By the time I made my second pilgrimage to the Holy land in 1985 Petra had a hotel, and shops and cafes had sprung up on the tarmac strip through the desert. The Israelis had also decided, in the interest of tourism, to relax the entry formalities and I felt comfortable taking my mother with me. My cousin, Dan Murphy, a deacon in the diocese of Toronto, and his wife Jean came from their home in Canada to join the pilgrimage; it was a valuable opportunity for us to spend time together. The Palestinians and Israelis were getting on a little better then and it was consequently easier to concentrate on the real reason we had come: to make a Christian pilgrimage. The places are more memorable the second time and embody more strongly the events which occurred at each one.

Unfortunately, on my third pilgrimage in 1989 most of us became very ill. It was almost certainly due to our eating bread freshly baked in an oven at the entrance to an outdoor café where we had stopped for lunch. The baker was needing the dough by throwing it from hand to hand. I am sure this is how so many of us were affected. Mother did not have any of this bread and so escaped, together with only six others. The rest of us ended up in bed. I was sharing a room with Father Jim Pannett; we certainly got to know each other very well during our illness. For at least four days something was trying to escape from every pore and opening in our bodies. Our bedclothes were permanently wet. The only remedy was to drink large amounts of water and keep taking the tablets given to us by one of our fellow knights, Alan Rebello, an Indian doctor who did a masterly job of looking after us day and night. How he got the tablets in sufficient quantity I never discovered. He refused to notify the authorities and get us into hospital because he was convinced we would be safer under his care. Only a few were not free of the germ by the time we went home, and they did not need hospital treatment.

On another occasion I was asked by Robert Benson, our representative on the Grand Magisterium of the Order, whether I would go out to Karack in Jordan to inspect a large secondary school being built with money we were providing. I was thrilled to have the chance and soon found a slot in my diary to go to Jerusalem. I was accommodated in a good hotel and the Vicar General drove me out to the site. Here I found the building work was only just coming out of the ground, but it still held some surprises. The site was tidy and well organised. The concrete was mixed in a large mixer and pumped to the places it was needed. Two men were already cutting the stone to be used for walling out of larger blocks, and the amount of finished blocks was already significant. I was told that these two men would provide all the stone for the walls. I would very much like to have continued monitoring the work but I was replaced by an Italian architect.

In the centenary year I went on a pilgrimage with the Order to Rome, where all the Lieutenancies were well represented. We filled St Peter's and the procession was almost the length of the Via della Conciliazione, the long road that leads up to St Peter's from the Castel Sant'Angelo. We made an impressive sight in our chivalric mantles, white with a red cross for the men and black with a red cross for the women. The idea of the whole Order going on pilgrimage was repeated two years later when we went to Lourdes. It was my first visit to this famous shrine of Our Lady and another of the experiences that have strengthened my faith.

The Military and Hospitaller Order of St Lazarus of Jerusalem

I do not think it wholly consistent with the concept of a religious Order to belong to more than one of them but I do not agree with those who refuse to accept that the Order of St Lazarus, being an ecumenical Order, is a valid exception. Investiture in the Order, which is under the protection of the Greek Melkite Patriarch of Antioch and All the East, of Alexandria and Jerusalem, is open to all practising Christians, and some of its Catholic members are also knights of the Holy Sepulchre. Many of its Church of England members are also members of the Venerable Order of St John. The present Grand Master of the Order is His Excellency, The Most Honourable Don Carlos Gereda de Borbon, Marqués de Almazán, a Catholic, and the Grand Prior of the Grand Priory of England and Wales is currently The Most Honourable the Marquis of Lothian, also a Catholic.

I was approached at the time Cardinal Hume was made an Honorary Joint Chaplain of the Grand Priory with the Archbishop of Canterbury and it was hoped that the Order would thus find even greater acceptance within the Catholic Church in England. I think it has achieved this acceptance, and the number of Catholic members has increased. The recently retired Chancellor, Chevalier Vincent Keaveny, is one.

When a new member is proposed, his faith as a Christian has to be established beyond doubt. I do not know what proportion of the membership is Roman Catholic. It is certainly greater in Europe; in England the majority of members would appear to be Anglican, but other Christian traditions are represented: Lutherans, Methodists and both Eastern and Oriental Orthodox.

The services are based on liturgy common to all Christian faiths and are directed by clergy of all faiths. The last investiture I attended was in the Cathedral of Saints Peter & Paul in Llandaff, Cardiff, the seat of the Anglican Archbishop of Wales. The service was presided over by the acting Dean of that cathedral but led by a Catholic priest, assisted by Catholic and Anglican clergy, while an excellent sermon was preached by a Methodist minister. Those being invested that day were mixed: lay men and women, clergy, young and old, and of all traditions.

There is more emphasis on the word of God in speech and music than we are used to and I find the change very prayerful. I also gain spiritual strength from being with people of other Christian faiths believing in, and praying to, the same God.

In England & Wales the Order of St Lazarus has its own national charitable trust that is separate from the management of the Order. This makes our donating more real and immediate, especially as we all have an opportunity to serve on the trust for a maximum of two three year periods. At the time of writing I am in my second term as a trustee.

CHAPTER 42

India

I was talking to Mike Warner one Friday evening over a pint in The Angel about the countries we would like to visit. Mike was keen to see India but there was no way his wife Laura could be tempted to join him. She does not like flying. He wanted to know if I would go with him. He had come across a brochure for a cruise around the coast of India. It was very expensive but there was a considerable discount if one allowed the company to choose the itinerary. This, of course, allowed them to fill cruises that would otherwise be under subscribed. Mike was confident that he could obtain the discount for the cruise we wanted by offering to take up places if it was under subscribed a month before it was due to start. I said I was happy to take the gamble with him. The company did not give us a positive answer but they took our details and we waited to receive a call. It came just before the Christmas holiday in 1996. We could have the cruise we wanted on Swan Hellenic's *Minerva*, leaving on Sunday 26th January 1997.

We flew to Singapore to join the ship. Our en suite cabins with showers were small but very good. I was particularly impressed with the shelf of books on India and the ability to see where we were going and where we had been on the television screen. We were also able, on our television set, to view the lectures being given in the lounge, the film being shown in the cinema, as well as television programmes. One could do almost everything lying down.

Although the *Minerva* was a small ship holding only 350 passengers, it had all the facilities one could want – with the emphasis on relaxation rather than exercise. There was a smoking room and a well stocked library with easy chairs – they called it 'country house style'. The six lecturers were very good. Sir John Ure had been with the Foreign Service in most parts of the world and ended his working life as ambassador in Cuba, Brazil, and Sweden. Dr Donald Stadtner, an associate professor at the University of Texas, was an expert on Indian art and sculpture, and Gerhard Bowering, the professor of Islamic studies at Yale, was excellent on religion in India.

All meals were available from a buffet, half inside the ship and half out on deck, or in a more formal dining room with waiter service. The dining room was, for the most part, furnished with large tables and one was directed to one's place at the next of these tables to be filled. Unless you arrived at the dining room with people you already knew, you could find yourself sitting with different people at every meal. The largest group of passengers were elderly folk who had spent much of their lives working overseas, now taking an opportunity to return and indulge in a little nostalgia. I have never before or since spent so much holiday time with so many people who had lived such interesting lives. They made excellent dinner companions and our conversation ranged over history, art, religion and politics. We tended to have breakfast and lunch in the buffet, but we always had dinner in the restaurant. One evening we avoided the large tables because Mike was not feeling up to making conversation. We asked for the smallest table they had and were shown to two empty seats at the only table for four in the restaurant. Subsequently, we were joined by the editor of *The Lady,* a magazine my mother used to read, and her friend. They were both rather younger than the average passenger and we enjoyed the change.

Our first attempt at sightseeing was a bus tour of Singapore. This was my first taste of Asia. It is very different from anywhere else I have been, and yet you can still see the influence of the British. In the evening we had one of the best meals I have eaten in the open, down on Clarke Quay. We were given a clay cooking pot with broth over a fire and a choice of fish and shell fish to cook ourselves. It tasted wonderful.

The following day we went to the Botanic Gardens to see the amazing display of orchids and had a drink in the famous Raffles Hotel. From Singapore we sailed to Kuala Lumpur in Malaysia where my brother had been stationed during their troubles. I wondered whether he had ever visited the Batu caves, where the important Hindu festival of Thaipusam, attended by over a million worshippers, had been held just before we arrived. Enormous quantities of elaborate and colourful paper decorations had been swept up into piles, waiting to be taken away. They added colour to the thirty foot wide staircase cut into the limestone mountain, home to a large number of small monkeys (macaques) scampering around the climbers in the hope of being fed. This staircase with its 272 steps, equivalent to over fourteen storeys, took us to the lower cave. Most people remain in this cave, which is where the Hindu effigies are and where the festival was held. Mike, who is younger and fitter than myself, insisted that we take the next fifty-four steps to the top cave. I rather think that the clarity of my memory was sharpened more by the effort required than the delight experienced.

The next day was memorable for a different reason. We were taken to the penal colony at Port Blair on the Andaman Islands, where the British detained Indian freedom fighters and criminals. The conditions were poor, but it is the writing on the walls and the heat that makes the conditions frightening. The gallows are still there, in a position that the inmates could not fail to see during their exercise periods. This added to the feeling of horror that pervades the place.

Our introduction to India was at Paradip in the early evening. Ours was the only ship docked in the small harbour which had been used for the unloading of coal, so the dockside was black with coal dust. The first visitors were the immigration officials, dressed in smart, well pressed white uniforms with gold epaulettes. Then came a military band, all wearing similarly well pressed white uniforms with gold buttons and epaulettes, who stood in the coal dust and played for us for about half an hour. A little later we received other officials, also dressed in white. The following morning we were driven by coach to Bhubaneshwar, a journey of over two hours, without seeing a single home that looked as if it could possibly have housed those immaculate uniforms.

The rest of our tour in India was a maze of temples and wide, overcrowded roads teeming with people, cows and traffic, all mixed up in an unbelievably slow shuffle – wonderful to behold but difficult to remember in detail. What I do recall are the very beautiful first class hotels we would visit for lunch during our tours. Mike and I were rather more active than most and thus able to secure the better tables when we stopped. This had been noticed by the daughter of Sir John and Lady Ure, who asked us to save them a place at a table in the hotel we were going to lunch in one day. We happened to enter the hotel in conversation with Lord and Lady Carrington and ended up sitting next to them at one end of a long trestle table in a marquee on the hotel lawn. We saved the seats on the other side of us for the Ures. They knew the Carringtons, but the atmosphere was rather strained and the Ures talked almost exclusively to other guests. When I later mentioned this apparent coolness, their daughter explained that when Lord Carrington was Foreign Secretary he had been responsible for appointing her father to Cuba, and he had still not forgiven him. I know how he felt. I had once found myself on a ferry going to Holland with someone I knew whom I seemed unable to avoid, although I was anxious to do so.

The cruise ended in Colombo, Sri Lanka, where, with the help of the excursion assistant, we were able to hire a car for the day to visit the site of Mike's friend's house. As we were leaving town the driver stopped at a temple and placed money in a container on the railings in front of it. This was a reminder of the dangers of driving north in those days. It was a long drive through unoccupied country to the site in a forest clearing at the top of a cliff. The house was already taking shape and, after taking photographs, we climbed down the stairs cut into the cliff to the secluded private beach. There was no other habitation in sight. 'A really delightful spot for someone else to enjoy,' I thought, 'but much too secluded for me.' On the way back we had a pot of tea to celebrate our visit to Ceylon, sitting in raffia chairs with our driver, on the terrace of a first class hotel and feeling very much as if we were in a scene from a film about the British Raj. We then drove back to Colombo. When we reached the temple we had stopped at on the way out, our driver pulled up again and placed more money in the same box on the temple railings. I asked him why. "That was to thank the Gods for keeping us safe," he replied.

CHAPTER 43

Rotary International

It was suggested to me in the early years of the practice that I should join the Rotary Club and the Chamber of Commerce, as membership would enable me to meet local business men who might make future clients. I thought it was a good idea but I was already involved in many Catholic social organisations and my partner, Ron Gillings, had yet to begin bringing work into the practice, so I persuaded Ron to join Rotary and the office joined the Chamber. He very much enjoyed the social life that Rotary provided and he would occasionally take me with him to the lunches. On one occasion I went with the club for a weekend in Bruges and liked the town so much that I have returned for many weekend breaks.

The Rotary lunches were very useful. Ron obtained quite a few commissions through meeting fellow Rotarians and many of the directors of the companies who used our services became well known to me: Price and Rankin, the glass people; Bent, in plant hire; Range, in transport; Don Orchard, in printing, and Roger Goodman, in property. We also consulted Norman Brooker of Sturt and Tivendale on property matters, and he was party to the purchase of our offices in Highgate. When Ron's daughter, Katharine, qualified and gained some experience in landscape gardening we helped her get started in a practice called 'cHOROS Landscape Architects' and became her partners. Ron introduced Katharine to Rotary when they started to accept women. She enjoyed being in it with her father but left after he died and she moved out of London.

When Ron died I lost track of the Rotarians, except for Don Orchard who continued to do our printing and Norman Brooker whom I had reason to contact occasionally. He was always trying to persuade me to join and when the Rotary Club of Islington, Highgate, and Muswell Hill began meeting at the Highgate Golf club in the evening rather than lunch time, I ran out of reasons for refusing.

The Rotarians in this group are a strange social mix of occupations, religions and physical types. We have members of the retail trades, bank managers, and other local professionals. We have Jews, Catholics, Orthodox, Anglicans and Muslims, men and women, married and single, and we range in age from forty to eighty; yet there are only twenty-one of us. Some are very tolerant, others less so. For some it is the most important part of their social life, for others it takes second place to supporting their football club. Some get very involved in the money raising activities and the competitive inter-club sports, others seem to do very little. Nobody seems to mind and we all get on well together. What is even more extraordinary is that the club distributes more than £12,000 every year to various local charities. They achieve this with their annual art exhibition and sale, their quiz night, and their Christmas collections. These last are made over six to eight nights for some two to three hours each night, and involve running after Father Christmas and a sleigh around the houses; three days are also spent standing with Father Christmas in the Islington, Highgate and Muswell Hill shopping centres. All this, of course, takes place during one of the coldest months of the year.

The charities we support are certainly deserving, but some

are more emotionally rewarding than others. I am particularly attracted to 'Treehouse' for autistic children and the Peter Rigby Trust for children with Down's syndrome, and I enjoy visiting them. Such visits make the money we personally give to these charities more meaningful. The Peter Rigby Trust will be my special charity when I become president of Rotary this year. This will mean trying to be more involved than I have managed to be in the past but it is the least I can do to repay them for their most delightful company. I have already agreed to spend a long weekend with twelve of them at the Eastbourne district conference.

CHAPTER 44

Marriage

As a workaholic, I must admit I have difficulty in maintaining emotional relationships. They tend, with very few exceptions, to start during the slack times and peter out when I get busy. Then one has to start all over again. In this context I have often resorted to advertising. In my mid-twenties my brother and I tried to place an advertisement in *The Times* for girls to share the costs of motoring holidays with us in Europe. That august newspaper refused to publish it unless we substituted 'girls' with the word 'companions'. How society has changed since then!

In my forties I answered adverts for singles holidays, and in more recent times I have written, and answered, adverts for friendship and marriage. The last I answered was:

Fiona. Age 56, very tall, short hair, always dressed in black, living in Harrow, working in Public Relations and interested in the theatre and travel.

I gave her a call. She sounded pleasant and business-like. We agreed to meet early in January 2003, but she cancelled this arrangement, saying she would call again. I assumed she was not interested and was surprised when some weeks later she did phone again. The excuse she gave for having cancelled struck me as weak; nevertheless, I reluctantly agreed to meet her at The Flask in Highgate at one o'clock on Sunday, 23rd February 2003. I was due to have lunch at 2.30 with my mother, who lived some fifteen minutes' drive from The Flask. It was cold but beautifully sunny.

When I reached the pub even the forecourt was crowded and I had to wait till past one o'clock for a table. I then had to fend off other people to avoid having to share. It was nearly half past one when I got a mobile call to say she was held up by road works on North Hill. When she arrived, five minutes later, I was irritable. She looked very nice, however, and I was pleased to ask her what she wanted to drink. By this time the pub was even more crowded and, going inside, I saw there was a very long queue at the bar. Conscious of the time, I returned and suggested we went for a coffee at a nearby restaurant in Pond Square. She agreed and we were at least able to talk to each other while walking to the restaurant. She excused herself for being late, but then claimed that I had helped to create the problem by having agreed to an arrangement whilst knowing I would have to leave shortly for lunch. It was not the ideal start to a friendship and when, after some twenty minutes, I had to prepare to depart, she expressed surprise that I suggested meeting again. She was even more concerned that I proposed meeting in yet another pub – but she accepted.

I arrived at The Prince of Wales a little early to find a couple I knew were there. Rather unwisely, I joined them in conversation. After only a few minutes Michael Warner, whose friends they were, came in and joined us. By the time Fiona arrived we were deep in conversation. I realised I had no alternative but to introduce her. It was then difficult to break away. In fact, they were making a good job of getting to know her. It was quite late by the time I got her out of the pub and into the San Carlo restaurant. I remarked that she had got on very well with my friends but had virtually ignored me. She, on the other hand, was not a little upset that I had agreed to meet her in a pub where I was almost sure to encounter acquaintances of mine. However, by the end of the evening we had become good friends.

Some fifteen months after meeting Fiona I was interviewing candidates wishing to study for the priesthood at Allen Hall. A lad with a very self-confident attitude, answered a question on celibacy with, "What would you know about marriage?" He was basing his knowledge on the gossip he had picked up from other students in the seminary about my bachelor state. I told him he should be more careful as information from such sources could quickly become out of date. That evening, after dinner, we were having a drink in the bar when the Vocation Director, Father Chris Vipers, approached and asked whether I was getting married. I was amazed because we had not yet told anyone. I asked how he knew and he replied that one of the candidates had said I was. I felt I had to give in. Within days this bit of gossip, with the help of the priests of the diocese, reached almost everyone I knew. Not surprising really: this was my first marriage and I was seventy-four.

I had not realised just how interested everyone would be in my bride-to-be. They all asked why I had left it so long, and how I had met her – a pleasant change from "Why have you never got married?"

The marriage took place on the 17th June 2005 in my local parish church of St Joseph. The principal concelebrant was my friend Canon Kevin, together with Father Daniel, the parish priest, and Father Tom, an American past president of Serra who was also a great friend. They were assisted by Deacon Dan Murphy, my cousin from Canada. My best man was Brian Hartigan.

At the appointed time we were all silently seated in our

places waiting for my bride to arrive. After about fifteen minutes our guests started to talk to each other and by the time Fiona arrived, some forty minutes late, the noise resembled a party in which even the clergy were involved, while most of the congregation were wandering about talking to each other. Fiona was given away by her brother, Peter; her two daughters, Gemma and Alice, were her bridesmaids. They made a very attractive procession. It was an extremely happy wedding and we were both much more emotional than I had expected us to be.

The reception for about 100 was held in Lauderdale House in Waterlow Park, only the width of a road away from the church. The house is where Nell Gwyn, the famous mistress of Charles II, is said to have lived briefly in 1670. The buffet was indoors but we could wander out onto the terrace to enjoy lovely views of the park. The sun shone all afternoon and everyone was delighted. The speeches following the cutting of the cake would not have warranted a mention were it not for an unscheduled and unrehearsed speech from my eldest step-daughter, Gemma. She welcomed me into the family with great feeling. In the evening there was dancing to a small band, the musicians ably assisted by Fiona's brother and his wife, Monty and Marsha, who are professional guitarists and singers of American folk songs. They combined with the official band to create a jam session as we left in the Mercedes at 10.00 pm to spend the night in a small hotel in Rosslyn Hill, Hampstead. The following day we returned the car to our flat and picked up our luggage for the flight to Bangkok, where we were attending the Serra International Convention before our great week's honeymoon in a chalet at Koh Samui, a beautiful island just off the coast of Thailand.

Fiona's flat was sold and the money used to purchase one in The Miltons, Highgate, for Alice, who was nineteen when we got married. It is only a twenty-five minute walk from ours. Her sister, Gemma, who was twenty-nine at the time, has a flat in Hackney so it is easy for either (or both) of them to join us for a meal.

I am now several years older and enjoying the many pleasures of sharing my life with someone I love. Our lives have knitted together perfectly and it is a surprise to find how many times we meet during the day to advise and help each other. I have redesigned the flat to convert one of our bedrooms into an office for Fiona. It still has a bed in it if someone needs to stay, and I have converted the smaller flat into an office-cum-guest room – so we have plenty of space for ourselves and guests.